Unwin Education Books: 31

THE SECOND 'R'
Writing Development in the Junior School

Unwin Education Books

Series Editor: Ivor Morrish, BD, BA, Dip.Ed. (London), BA (Bristol)

Unwin Education Books: 31
Series Editor: Ivor Morrish

The Second 'R'

Writing Development in the Junior School

WILLIAM HARPIN
B.A., M.Ed.
School of Education, University of Nottingham

London   George Allen & Unwin Ltd
Ruskin House   Museum Street

First published in 1976

ISBN 0 04 372018 8 hardback
     0 04 372019 6 paperback

Composition, in 10 point Times Roman
by Linocomp Ltd, Marcham, Oxfordshire
Printed in Great Britain
by Biddles Ltd, Guildford, Surrey

For Rita

Acknowledgements

Writing a book is, in the end, a solitary labour, but this one rests on the efforts of so many individuals that my sense of indebtedness will be only feebly discharged in attempting to give formal, though deeply-felt recognition here for their labour, advice and encouragement. For what I have made of our collective endeavours, the ultimate responsibility is mine, but I hope they will see some worthwhile reflection of their hopes in what follows.

Pride of place needs to be given to the richly diverse group of children who allowed writing, on which they had lavished much care, to disappear forever from their sight, and who furthered my education so cheerfully. To their teachers I am grateful for their willingness to take on extra burdens and for their tolerant acceptance of an alien presence in their classrooms. I learnt much from discussions with them and with the head teachers of their schools, whose unstinting support for the enquiry was so freely given, and vital to its completion. Of my fellow workers on the project, I owe most to Don Smedley of Loughborough College of Education for his immense labours on the linguistic analysis, to Jack Williamson of Eaton Hall College of Education who began the whole enterprise and was a resourceful solver of difficulties throughout, and to Janet Ede (Matlock College of Education) and Susan Hescott, née Nott (formerly of Chilwell Comprehensive School) for their writing classification system, reproduced in Chapter 5. A host of teachers in the Midlands, London and the South, in discussing the results and conclusions on a variety of in-service courses, contributed greatly to clarifying a number of the issues; I hope I have done justice to their many ideas in the text. The financial support of the Social Science Research Council was vital in allowing us to extend the scope of the enquiry well beyond its first modest limits and I gratefully acknowledge that help.

I offer my thanks to the following for permission to reproduce copyright and other material:

to Dr Malcolm Schonell for the children's writing from his father's *Backwardness in the Basic Subjects*, used in Chapter 4;
to Macmillan and Co. for the extract from 'The Circus Animals' Desertion' by W. B. Yeats, in Chapter 5;

to Professor J. N. Britton for material derived from a briefing document on his system of categories for a functional description of writing (and for much good advice too);

to Don Measham, of Matlock College of Education, for the extract from Roy's autobiography, used in Chapter 5 (first printed in his *Fourteen*, Cambridge University Press, 1965);

to Colin Harrison for the 'A good story – but not much history' illustration, employed in Chapter 3.

My final debt is to Mary Durkan, for her skill in converting steadily deteriorating handwriting so accurately into typescript.

Contents

Tables

1
Introduction

'We need to ask more often of everything we do in school, "Where are we trying to get, and is this thing we are doing helping us to get there?" '
(John Holt – *How Children Fail*)

Asking questions and attempting to discover answers to them are activities at the centre of both learning and teaching. Much of a child's early learning, often to the exasperation of his parents, is a seemingly inexhaustible succession of experiments, physical and verbal, to make satisfying sense of the world he is in. A teacher, too, is impelled to employ similar methods in an attempt to understand the whole process he is engaged in. A powerful, wide-ranging curiosity is fundamental to both roles; without it the learner makes no advances, the teacher relies more and more heavily on the mechanical application of ready-made solutions.

There is, of course, nothing startlingly new or revolutionary in this. At a time when discontent was beginning to mount about the effects of 'payment by results' on learning and teaching, in the early 1880s, Professor Armstrong advocated with some success what he called the 'heuristic' method of teaching science. In essence this was a form of discovery learning, in which the pupil was placed in the position of the original investigator, faced his problems, formulated questions, tested hypotheses and began to piece together a living understanding of scientific principles. Though Armstrong's methods were warmly supported by the British Association, teachers were less enthusiastic, partly perhaps because it represented such a radical change in their function, but more because child and scientist could not be said to occupy the same starting point. Only in recent years has educational practice begun seriously to take account of the principle underlying Armstrong's experiments: that teaching is an enabling process, creating conditions in which a child can develop his understanding of experience in the most effective ways possible. The 'discovery' method, individualised learning, topic work, project-based teaching, integrated day organisation, family grouping are reflections in organisation and method of the principle; changes in the curriculum to take account of it have occurred most notably in mathematics and the sciences, but inter-disciplinary experiment is affecting the traditional humanities subjects more and more.

If children are increasingly being allowed and encouraged to be active in discovering their own understandings, what of the teachers? Most would agree that identifying problems and testing solutions to them are vital to their business. Equally, those same teachers would point to a formidable array of obstacles preventing these processes from occurring in anything more than a fragmentary way. Quite apart from over-large classes and over-burdened timetables, coping with absences and adjust-ing to organisational changes, one obstacle is more unscalable than most others. For all but the most immediate questions (and not always for these), the evidence on which to base possible solutions is incomplete. Teachers become remarkably adept at using intuition, inspired guess-work and imaginative inference to produce answers, but the procedure is wasteful of time and energy for those who can ill-afford either.

One solution to this dilemma is to find ready-made answers elsewhere. The Schools Council, particularly on curriculum change and develop-ment, has been an invaluable source in recent years. More generally, educational research has been expected to offer this kind of help. Its findings, though, are not always accessible and the questions it seeks to explore not necessarily those exercising teachers most frequently and urgently.

The work reported on in this book arose as an attempt to find a more direct way of encouraging teachers to ask questions and to participate directly in the efforts to discover answers to them.

In 1966, a group of college of education lecturers met to discuss the state of English language teaching in schools, intending to prepare a research enquiry. Two conclusions emerged very quickly from those early meetings: the group needed time to inform itself more fully of the current state of the art, and teachers from a full range of schools were vitally necessary additions for fulfilling the group's original aims.

The year was significant, though this was not apparent at the time. It represented, in English teaching, a pause between early efforts at establishing new directions and emphases in a variety of areas and the still-continuing attempts to consolidate those ideas and to spread them more widely among teachers. Examinations had been under scrutiny: 'O' level language had been found wanting (*The Examining of English Language* 1964); CSE courses in English were taking the first tentative steps towards an independent existence. 'Oracy' had become a topic of study and concern, as a result of the work of Wilkinson and others (in 1965), but the implications were still being digested. Children's writing, under the banner of the 'creative' writing movement, was being taken seriously and it is possible to see *The Excitement of Writing* (Clegg 1964) as a definitive statement of its new position. It was the year of the Dartmouth Seminar, at which English and American teachers argued productively over the state of English teaching and ways of improving it (admirably reported in John Dixon's *Growth through English* in 1967).

With the generous assistance of their employing authorities, the group, now a working party of lecturers and teachers twenty-six strong, embarked on a programme of self-education. Distinguished speakers were invited to describe and interpret the latest advances in linguistics, in the psychology and sociology of language and in explorations of their applications to the classroom. The group also sought to learn from research and development enquiries then in being, and was fortunate in being able to forge links with the Schools Council project at University College, London, acting as a development centre for the materials which later became *Breakthrough to Literacy* and *Language in Use*. The group drew widely on the experience and expertise of its own members to explore the implications of this range of enquiries for children talking and listening, reading and writing.

The research proposal which eventually emerged from these proceedings was very different from that envisaged at the start. In a real sense, the participants had used the opportunity to re-examine their teaching problems, to distinguish profitable from unprofitable areas, questions from pseudo-questions and to estimate with some accuracy the strengths and limitations of different approaches in the search for answers. Even so, with so large and varied a group, no one was surprised to find a great range of suggestions put forward to provide a focus for the members' efforts.

The first idea was to study intensively the development of a range of language abilities in children aged 6, 8, 10 and 12 in an attempt to track down the causes of the enormous variations in language skills. A great variety of other proposals followed, reflecting the range of teaching interests represented by the contributing teachers. They included:

(1) an investigation of the relationship between speech and writing;
(2) the evaluation and assessment of children's written work;
(3) the standards of English encouraged by textbooks, the status of the 'rules' they offer and the language in which they are expressed;

(4) the effects of the media, particularly television, in a child's language;
(5) the relationship between auditory and visual perception and language learning;
(6) the problem of 'language deficit';
(7) the effectiveness of direct teaching techniques for certain language skills (spelling, punctuation, sentence structure);
(8) creativity and language;
(9) the way in which children learn to fit their language to different situations;
(10) language skills and reading.

The final choice among these rival possibilities was a difficult one for the group to make. Each had enthusiastic advocates for its intrinsic interest and its importance to teachers. In reaching a decision, group members applied a series of tests to each idea. How well was the group equipped with the specialist skills demanded? For a lengthy study, was the group able to guarantee its own stability? Was there a possibility of wasteful overlap with the efforts of other groups? Would the school and teaching resources of members be fully made use of? What difficulties would there be in formulating a workable design for the enquiry?

After these processes had been applied, a favoured theme had emerged : the development of writing in the junior school. A detailed plan was then prepared which took into account the possibility of attracting financial support for the work; assistance for this was generously provided by the Social Science Research Council.

Four interlocking objectives determined the shape of the final proposal :

(1) to study the language resources displayed in writing by children of widely-differing abilities in the junior school, and to follow the order and manner of development of those resources over a period of two years;
(2) to attempt to explain observed differences by reference to elements in school-writing situations, teaching methods and organisation, the language exchanges of teachers and pupils, school resources, the expectations of both teachers and schools;
(3) to attempt an estimate of the influence of the wider social context on this development – the nature of the local community, socio-economic status, parents' educational aspirations for their children, size of family and the child's position in it;
(4) to derive from this evidence suggestions for more effective educa-

tional practice in developing written language skills and in recognising and overcoming difficulties in writing.

The nine schools which took part in the investigations varied widely in geographical location, size, age and in the catchment areas they served. Fifty teachers in them collaborated with the group in devising situations for writing, offering information on their procedures, allowing observers into their classrooms and making available a mass of information derived from their knowledge of the pupils involved. A sample of three hundred children, designed to be representative by age, sex, ability and social-class membership of the whole junior school population aged 7.0 to 9.11, was selected and their progress in writing followed through two school years. Questionnaires were completed by head teachers on their schools and by teachers on themselves, their teaching situations, their methods and on each of the pupils chosen for the enquiry. The children provided four pieces of writing in each of the six terms to a pattern that would permit inter-class and inter-school comparisons without asking for major changes in the way that writing was normally undertaken. In addition a detailed schedule of observations was prepared in order to study the children in their classroom setting, concentrating on their patterns of behaviour and characteristic ways of working. This was used three times during the two years, offering a dynamic view of events to complement the essentially static information from other sources.

The shape of the writing programme was not arrived at without some false starts. Attempts to collect all the writing produced on one or several days proved unsatisfactory. With so great a variety of patterns of work, no day could be said to be 'typical' and the writing element was completely unpredictable. Much was not the child's own, in the sense of coming from work cards, text-books, reference works, and it was often impossible to decide where the borrowed stretches of language began and ended.

The solution adopted was to select two dimensions on which writing could be varied. The first of these, well understood by the teachers taking part, was the distinction of kind, between 'creative' and 'factual' writing, or, using other labels, 'personal' and 'recording'. The second dimension related to preparation for writing; on the one hand 'minimum' on the other 'full' or 'extensive', with regard to verbal preparation. So, of the four pieces of writing in each term, two would be creative, two factual; within each, one would be verbally fully prepared, the other undertaken with the least possible preliminary discussion. This was a challenge to the teachers, particularly for the category 'factual, with minimum verbal preparation', a rare writing event in the experience of most. Their resourcefulness in meeting these demands was, in the event, of a very high order.

At the end of the two years, apart from all the other information, more than 6,600 separate pieces of writing had been accumulated, nearly 1,700 in each of the four writing categories. Our group of child writers had produced an inspiring (or daunting) 800,000 words of evidence and the task of analysing and interpreting had to begin.

What follows is based on an attempt to understand the implications of some of that evidence. It would be foolish to claim that all the original questions have been answered : some answers have inevitably given rise to a new host of questions; some early questions remain as puzzling as ever. Much of the material still awaits detailed exploration, but enough has emerged to encourage this attempt to share both the discoveries and the uncertainties.

2

The Purposes of Writing

'By maintaining the written word as the keystone of our education, we are opting for political and social stasis.'
(Neil Postman – *The Politics of Reading*)

'Only phonetic writing has the power to translate man from the tribal to the civilised sphere, to give him an eye for an ear.'
(Marshall McLuhan – *The Gutenberg Galaxy*)

Writing is one of those taken-for-granted accomplishments in the social and cultural life of human beings. In developed societies literacy, the ability to read and to write, has been treated as a vitally important index of well-being. The progress of developing societies is frequently measured by it; the achievement of universal literacy a fundamental educational objective. Conversely, in those societies with a long history of literate education, evidence of illiteracy is the signal for great public concern and, as often as not, a flurry of activity designed to eliminate presumed faults in the educational system.

As the quotations at the head of this chapter show, the unquestioning acceptance of the importance of reading and writing is beginning to be challenged. McLuhan's argument is that the new mass media, particularly radio, cinema and television, have radically and permanently altered the processes of communication. The era which began with Gutenberg's use of movable type to create a print-dominated world is, he asserts, coming rapidly to a close. A new electronic era is under way. Reading and writing in the evolving world will be at best optional extras, perhaps finally obsolete. While McLuhan sees this as an inescapable process, he does not take sides and expresses no views on whether the change will be necessarily beneficial. Postman, by contrast, argues that the reign of print has been oppressive, by the effects that it has had on social organisation. The virtue of writing or print, its ability to transcend time, has a countervailing disadvantage; nothing need ever be lost. The weight of the past presses more and more heavily on the present, making change enormously difficult to initiate.

This argument, like the electronic age that gave it impetus, is still relatively new and very far from being resolved. What is unarguable is that it has fundamental implications for educational practice, regardless of outcome. There are questions for which no obvious answers yet exist. If print does finally disappear, will writing necessarily follow it? Is it possible to conceive of the two modes of communication, by sound and symbol, co-existing? How far does the general case apply to specialised systems of notation (mathematics, music)?

Meanwhile, the two modes *do* co-exist and efforts in education have to take account of the inescapable fact that literacy is still seen to be crucially important. Nevertheless, the very existence of the debate suggests a need to explore what is uniquely significant in possessing the skills of writing and reading in the 1970s and, as a starting point, to trace their history in schools.

In the Middle Ages the Church was supremely the depository of culture; kings and commoners alike left the literate skills largely in the hands and minds of clerics, with Latin as their medium. Schools existed to perpetuate this tradition and the vernacular had no standing in religion, law, politics or literature. The change from a medieval to a modern world in the fifteenth and sixteenth centuries, identified by the terms Renaissance and Reformation, was neither abrupt nor smooth; causes are still much argued over. Effects are easier to isolate. The growth of nationalism enhanced the claims of the vernacular to be taken seriously for important purposes, though in some fields, law for instance, this was still contested as late as the eighteenth century. The break with Rome gave impetus in England to translations of the Bible, which by royal decree (and the power of printing) were made accessible to all. Cranmer's Prayer Book was another powerful boost for the vernacular. Though the secondary schools continued in the dominant classical tradition, the growing number of 'elementary' or 'petty' schools concentrated on the mother tongue. For the purposes of the new state, the ability to read was paramount; writing in these petty schools was only taught to those who could read 'competently well'. The natural order of the two skills was thus reinforced by circumstances. You can read without needing to write, but writing, in any real sense, is impossible without the ability to read what has been written.

The consequences of this differential emphasis were far-reaching: until this century, writing tended to be a poor relation, only narrowly exploited. While reading had to be developed to a relatively high level to cope with the central texts, writing often went no further than an ability to copy the letters of the alphabet in the schools for the poor. Perhaps the most significant achievement for elementary writing instruction was the ability to produce a signature, instead of making a mark. A need to make available to all the population the full range of writing skills and benefits was not fully felt until very recently; its expression may be read into the provisions of the 1944 Education Act relating to 'secondary' education for all.

The term that so neatly summarises the extent, and limitations, of elementary education, 'the three Rs', we owe, by a nice irony, to a man who was the butt of his contemporaries for his struggles with language. Sir William Curtis made money very successfully in fishing and banking, became Lord Mayor of London and an MP and inspired enough affection among his London constituents to be given a huge funeral procession on his death in 1829. London society saw him differently. In a periodical (*The Mirror of Literature, Amusement and Instruction*) published in the year before his death, an anonymous gossip-writer refers sneeringly to the 'eccentricities of his composition' and the 'absurdities' in his speech. These are illustrated by toasts he is alleged to have given at public dinners, among which, at a school, he asked his fellow-guests to drink to 'The three Rs – Reading, Writing and Rithmetic'. Conscious joke or unconscious slip, this was an inspired invention, as the phrase's continued currency still testifies.

The effects of the phrase, in appearing to define the content of popular education, were less fortunate. The State, entering the business of education with great reluctance in the 1840s, tended to see these elements not as the foundation of the educational process, but as its sum total. In his 1855 report on the elementary schools for which he was responsible, Matthew Arnold expressed this view clearly enough, but with a significant rider: 'Reading, writing and elements of arithmetic are the basic instruction for all children, but they are not enough for those with prospects in life.'

Not that even these 'basic' elements were well taught. In his thirty years as an inspector of elementary schools, Arnold returned again and again to the shortcomings of teachers and, perhaps more accurately, to the restrictions imposed on what they were encouraged to teach. The so-called 'Revised Code' of 1862 was principally designed to make instruction in the three Rs more efficient. Arnold was happy to report on one of its first benefits (in the report for 1863) in improving the quality of school reading books, but thereafter his opinion of its effects became increasingly critical. 'It is now found possible, by ingenious preparation, to get children through the Revised Code examination in reading, writing and ciphering, without their really knowing how to read, write and cipher' (1867 report, repeated in 1869). A system of payment by results for teachers naturally encouraged this sterile ingenuity. The writing test for children in Standard III at this time was to write, from dictation, a sentence from the same lesson of their reading book in which they had just been tested for reading proficiency. To illustrate his argument, Arnold quoted the examination failure rates for the three basic subjects: arithmetic 20 per cent, writing 7·7 per cent, reading 6 per cent.

Successive amendments to the Code, after the Education Act of 1870 had begun the final movement towards universal elementary education, left the three Rs virtually unchanged. Arnold said as much in a report near the end of his thirty years' service as inspector (in 1880). 'It may be said that there are at present but three obligatory subjects in our schools . . . reading, writing and arithmetic.' The content of writing instruction was little different from that of a century before: from simple mastery of a writing instrument to copy writing and then simple dictation. In the 1870s 'composition' made its first appearance as a subject, but only for children in Standard V upwards. This was in any case hardly as revolutionary a step as it might sound, since the pupils concerned were asked merely to write down from memory the substance of a story that had been read aloud to them.

There were teachers in those Victorian schools who encouraged children to go beyond these cripplingly narrow limits. One powerful example (evidently the work of a boy from an upper Standard in a London elementary school) is reproduced by Peter Armitstead in *English in the Middle Years*. Here is a fluent 1,000-word piece taking its inspiration from a day trip to Portsmouth. As Armitstead comments, it is a lively piece of personal writing, expressed honestly and without any fear of teacher reprisal. All the other evidence suggests, though, that this boy was one of a fortunate minority, lucky in his school and his teacher. Most children of the time, after laboriously acquiring the skill of making letters, would have used that skill solely for copying the words of others.

By the turn of the century, the elementary schools had achieved a degree of liberation for a variety of reasons. 'Payment by results' was gone and with it the annual examinations; 'higher-grade' elementary schools appeared with a broader curriculum; the quality of teaching was affected by entrants from the new day-training courses attached to universities and later from the newly-created municipal teacher-training colleges. As a result of the influence of curriculum reform in the secondary schools, English as such became a subject in elementary schools for the first time, though dominated by those tenacious (and still surviving) subdivisions – composition, grammar, handwriting, spelling, dictation, with literature offering opportunities for yet further categories.

The benefits for writing in these changes were, evidently, small. George Sampson in *English for the English*, written in 1921, reserved some of his most powerful invective for the state into which it had fallen. 'I have grown into a conviction that the usual school subject called "composition" is a mistaken and useless activity, wasting more time and effort than any subject in the curriculum ... I will crystallise my views in a sentence and say "Let us abolish composition from the curriculum." ' For Sampson the folly was in how the term was interpreted. Many teachers believed 'composition' and 'essay' to be identical and felt that exercise books should resemble the *Essays of Elia*, with only a modest allowance made for the age of the pupils involved. Exercises in a difficult, recondite literary form made no kind of educational sense to Sampson, whose solution foreshadows a much later development in schools. 'Everything they [the pupils] write is "composition"... We want students to understand that there are two kinds of writing, the statement and the creation : that ability to state is expected from them, but not ability to create, though we are ready to give them credit for genuine attempts at creation . . . It is towards the story and the play, and not towards the essay or composition that the creative activity of children can be most profitably directed.'

Sampson's influence is plain in a report from a committee appointed by the Board of Education to enquire into the state of English teaching, published as *The Teaching of English in England* in 1921. In both book and report the fundamental importance of speech was emphasised, a concern that has been translated into practice only in very recent times, but the state of writing caused the greatest uneasiness. 'The capacity for self-expression is essentially the measure of the success or failure of a school, at any rate on the intellectual side. If the habit of merely perfunctory or artificial writing is allowed to usurp its place, the avenue to mental development will have been partly closed' (report, section 76). Sampson's distinction of 'statement' and 'creation' kinds of writing in the schools found reflection in the critical comments of employers on the writing skills of school-leavers (complaints that have a very contemporary ring to them). 'Our candidates do not appreciate the value of shades of meaning, and while able to do imaginative composition, show weakness in work which requires accurate description or careful arrangement of detail' (section 77).

This report incorporated a variety of practical and sensible suggestions for improving writing in schools. The report of the Hadow Committee in 1931, *The Primary School*, showed little sign of their influence.

'Composition' and 'essay', terms that were treated with reserve and some suspicion in the earlier report, were still at the centre of discussion, but now apparently accepted as inevitable descriptions of the bulk of written work, even for younger pupils. This, together with a failure to consider the *purposes* of writing, reduced the effect of some laudable recommendations. 'Oral practice should not be sacrificed to the written essay.' 'The pupil must have something to say . . . upon incidents of home life, your children will write fully and naturally, and will desire to write.' 'In the course of the upper stage of primary education, care should be taken to include narrative, description, some exposition and, if possible, some argumentation.'

The confusion of thinking in the Hadow Report did not, of course, prevent individual teachers from attempting bold and imaginative experiments with writing. One nine-year-old in the late 1930s was encouraged to write a nativity play for his classmates and a two-exercise-book adventure story, read in instalments to an uncritical audience on Friday afternoons. For many though, the mixture as before remained : a solid diet of English exercises, spelling and dictation, with a weekly attempt to devise new adventures for a shilling in an instantly recognisable 'schoolteacher's English' prose style. Enquiries into the popularity of various school subjects during that decade discovered many of the staple English activities unflatteringly at the bottom of most lists for elementary school children; dictation, recitation, grammar and composition competed for the doubtful distinction of being 'least liked'. It is worth remembering that these elements of English work figured prominently in many selection tests for transfer from junior to selective secondary schools, with predictable effects on the curriculum for older children in junior schools. These influences were perhaps also responsible for the narrowness of vision imposed on teachers in responding to the writing they received. John Blackie's example (in *Good Enough for the Children?* 1963) is justly well known : a nine-year-old, faced with the standard composition title 'My Father', wrote what amounted to an elegy on his recently dead father. Comment? 'Tenses. You keep mixing past and present.'

In a later essay in the same book, Blackie suggested that the state of writing in schools had at last made significant progress. 'I have no hesitation in saying that the single most dramatic change for the better in primary education since the war has been in written work, that this change is seen in its most surprising manifestations in the upper infants' classes and that it is sufficiently widespread to be significant.' No amount of analysis will explain fully how, after so many years of stagnation, the change was brought about, but some important elements do stand out.

In 1954 the Ministry of Education issued pamphlet no. 26 – *Language: Some Suggestions for Teachers of English and Others.* The shift of teaching emphasis is marked, though the contents of the pamphlet would not in general have startled the authors of the 1921 report. After reviewing the disappointing progress of English teaching and remarking that 'it cannot, in fact, hoist itself up far by pulling in turn at the straps of its own boots', the authors offer a general proposition to point the way to a solution. 'No substantial and permanent progress is likely to take place until "English", literature as well as language, is regarded by all in authority as the central expression of English life and culture and as the central subject in the education of every English child of every age and every grade of intelligence.' A new place for English in the curriculum and the involvement of *all* teachers in its promotion: again the notions were not new, but the climate more propitious than ever before.

Two years later, the results of experiments with writing, extending over seven years, were published in modest format by the Bristol Institute of Education. The age of 'creative' writing had dawned, though Mrs Pym used the title 'Free Writing' as a more appropriate description of her techniques. This approach to writing was not new – individual teachers before this time undoubtedly tried it – but it seems to have been the first thorough, systematic attempt to explore its possibilities and to provide a rationale for its use. The change of emphasis was simple, but profound in its consequences. Instead of writing *about* something, children were asked to write *from* something. Subjects were replaced by starting-points; the closed 'composition' gave way to free exploration of experience.

The kinds of stimuli used by Mrs Pym in those early experiments have grown only too familiar in the two decades since: exploration of the senses, *objets trouvés*, fragments of poetry, paintings, constructions of no obvious utility. Just as important in their way were two innovations in method:

(1) the usual period of preparation for writing (by exposition, discussion, exchange of ideas, blackboard planning) was dispensed with;
(2) children were encouraged to be less anxious about the mechanics of writing, particularly spelling and punctuation.

Two pieces by Andrew, a ten-year-old in a Hampshire junior school, illustrate the effects of these changes. First, a traditional 'composition', on the title 'School', fully prepared and with the usual rules on spelling, punctuation and handwriting in force.

My School

'I think school is a very nice place. You learn a lot and it helps you to get a good job later on in life. If we didn't go to school the world would be very backward. When we are born and grow older it is up to us to learn.

'The school dinners are very tasty and nearly every day we have greens which help us to grow big and strong. The cooks and dinning room attendents are very nice.

'The teachers are very helpful at our school and we have a nice headmaster who hardly ever grumbles at us. I don't blame him if he did.

'The school hours are very well placed and unlike most schools we have 1½ hours for dinner. We have four playtimes. One when we come to school, one at 10.30 a.m., one at dinner time and one at 2.30 p.m.

'Our school surroundings are very beautiful and as we have lots of trees near us we see: birds, squirrels and there are horses in the field next to us. The Vicarage is very near and we go there to collect conkers as we are very fond of them.'

Three weeks later, as an experiment, Andrew and his classmates were taken to a derelict school nearby, allowed to wander round for twenty minutes, then went back to school and wrote about the experience:

The Old School

'Ivy hangs from the topmost windows like snakes hung upside down. It lashes out at your arms and tries to hold you back. Where once feet clattered and boys chattered moss grows. Where are the feet where have the boys gone forever from the warm fires. The swimming pool rusts every hour of the day Everything everywhere is going to dust in that cold lonely place. Water no more comes foreward from the taps no more do boys play with the soap Dormitorys are dull empty silent. A study stands gloomy and bare. The wind streams in every crack and cranny.'

Experiments with new ways of encouraging free, personal writing in schools, especially with younger children, began to grow rapidly. For the most part they were the work of individual teachers, deeply dissatisfied with the old prescriptions for writing. Margaret Langdon in *Let the Children Write* (published in 1961) described what prodded her into action. 'It all started with boredom – boredom and disappointment. I expect you would be bored by the time you had reached the end of the thirtieth essay . . . I mark one, then another, and yet another, scratching through the dumb phrases, the unimportant thoughts, the platitudinous expressions, and end with an unenthusiastic "Fair" and a private thought, "What's the use?" '

The new label, 'intensive', was coined by Mrs Langdon to take account of the special features she stressed: emotion, brevity, simplicity, honesty. Perhaps the most interesting technical innovation was to direct attention to form: each new idea was to occupy a new line of writing.

Margery Hourd (in *The Education of the Poetic Spirit* and *Coming into Their Own*) demonstrated very effectively the way in which the writing of poetry tapped otherwise unreachable areas in a child's experience. Poetry writing was a key too for Robert Druce (*The Eye of Innocence*) and Jack Beckett (*The Keen Edge*). David Holbrook (particularly in *English for the Rejected*) asserted the need for children to exercise the full 'poetic function': 'the capacity to explore and perceive, to come to terms with, speak of and deal with experience by the exercise of the whole mind and all kinds of apprehensions, not only intellectual ones'.

Of at least equal importance was the publication in 1964 of a fully annotated anthology of children's writing, edited by A. B. Clegg, *The Excitement of Writing*. Apart from the encouragement this offered to teachers to explore new ways of stimulating writing, it contained a brief but important statement on kinds of writing. Clegg distinguished 'personal' from 'recording' writing and in doing so drew attention to the need to take due account of both in devising programmes of writing. By this time, so-called 'creative' writing was beginning to dominate all discussions of the nature and place of writing, notably in primary schools. Counter-revolutionaries tended to see in it the cause of a supposed decline in general standards of competence in English. Arguments developed over its functions and its treatment by teachers. Some asserted its value as a psycho-therapeutic agent, releasing tension and anxiety and contributing to emotional development. Others used such writing, often with more ingenuity than sense, as the raw material for amateur essays in psychoanalysis. Much of the inspiration of the originators of the movement was lost, so that creative writing sessions became as formalised and sterile as the composition lessons they replaced.

Surprisingly little was made of this in the Central Advisory Council Report, *Children and Their Primary Schools* (the Plowden Report), when it appeared in 1967. It acknowledged the existence of 'creative' writing, advocated the use of a child's deeply felt experience as the best source material, and referred briefly to the value of varieties of recording writing. There seems more than a hint in these sections (601–13, Volume I) of superficiality in the committee's treatment of a complex area of learning and teaching; even perhaps a touch of complacency.

Most of these questions remain unanswered or overlooked, though, in the many excellent books on writing in schools which continue to appear, one or two of them have been acknowledged rather more fully than in the past, notably a concern with giving school writing a purpose. The more fundamental question posed at the beginning of this survey – what place do reading and writing have in today's world? – has had negligible attention, apparently lost to view in the welter of more obviously practical concerns.

WHY BOTHER WITH WRITING?

The arguments set out in this chapter so far, with their supporting evidence, amount, in the end, to one central proposition. We devote enormous resources to helping pupils achieve some kind of mastery of reading and writing without ever making explicit our reasons for the effort. They have been taken for granted; skills on which the rest of the educational process is founded. This has been the case despite the great changes in education itself, in the ends it is intended to serve and in the world its pupils have to live in. The current campaign to combat adult illiteracy is one more manifestation of this continuing concern. Many of the arguments for this latest effort are familiar echoes from the past, all of which coalesce into one. To live in this world without the capacity for reading and writing is to suffer a crippling disadvantage, making absurd any hope of equality of opportunity. But what do we need reading and writing for?

There can be no denying the usefulness, in a very practical sense, of being able to read in a society so heavily dependent on the printed word. Much, probably most, of the information we need comes in this form, despite the increasing emphasis on the pictorial. Though traffic signs convey their messages largely (but not exclusively) without language, they are given coherence for the road-user through the language-dominated Highway Code. Reading a book is not the most effective way of learning to drive a car, but to maintain and repair it properly there is no escape from the maker's handbook and workshop manual. Those who have tried to assemble or to operate machines, toys or household gadgets in the absence of printed instructions quickly come to recognise the usefulness of language. Official demands on the ability to read fluently and accurately multiply as society grows more complex, more participatory. The world is filled with forms, instructions, advice, regulations, exhortations, demands and a necessary body of experts to help the ordinary individual in his struggle with them. Often enough their advice has, at its centre, the warning 'read all the small print'.

If the case for reading is strong, that for writing is less obvious, despite their complementary nature. Certainly many of those forms have to be filled in, but the level of *writing* skill demanded, by contrast with reading, is generally elementary. The annual tax return is a searching test of higher skills in reading, but requires no eloquent written composition. For most tax-payers, routine copying, a signature and a date will suffice. Those with more complex tax problems employ a highly skilled reader/writer to carry the entire process through on their behalf; a situation closely resembling the medieval one described earlier.

There is, in fact, no comprehensive and systematic account of what we, in general, use writing for in our daily lives. Leaving aside those who, in one way or another, make their living by writing, what is the practical value of the skill to the rest of us? Writing letters, making notes to aid memory, providing signatures – the list of universal writing events is a short one. This is, of course, leaving out of account what might be called the non-utilitarian uses of writing: writing for its own sake, though even here technology, in the shape of the tape-recorder, can provide some sort of substitute for the diarist, poet, novelist or dramatist.

If this analysis is accepted at its face value, priorities in teaching are instantly recognisable. Speech comes first because, to quote Anshen, 'man is that being on earth who does not have language: man *is* language'. Without the ability to produce and receive language there can be no sense of community with others, as the plight of deaf children so obviously testifies. Reading, for the reasons advanced earlier, needs to be developed to a high level. For writing though, there is only a modest place and limited ambitions. Yet schools have, until quite recently, ordered their work to give priority to writing and reading, with speech a poorly-regarded third. Now that command of the spoken language is beginning to achieve its rightful place in educational practice, where should writing stand?

THE VALUE OF WRITING

This book would not need to exist if the face-value utility of writing were the sole justification for its place in the curriculum. There is more to it, but what that is needs to be carefully explored. The history of educational practice is uncomfortably full of examples of something being taught because it was there, or for reasons that would not bear a moment's close scrutiny. A relevant and instructive example was the domination of English language teaching by a grammar mistakenly based on Latin, which remained largely unchallenged for 150 years despite its obvious shortcomings.

First, it is helpful to establish how writing stands in relation to speech. They are two distinct modes of language, despite their fundamental identity. To encourage pupils, as teachers often have done, to 'write as you speak' is to ask the impossible. When we listen to someone speaking, we are exposed to a great deal of information which is not in the 'language' part of the communication at all. We are aware of voice quality, pronunciation, pace, emphasis, loudness, pausing. We note, and interpret, the physical attitude of the speaker, the situation in which the speech act is taking place and the role that we, as listeners, are supposed to be playing. All but a tiny part of this 'extra-linguistic' information vanishes when communication proceeds by writing, rather than speaking. There are writing conventions that try to re-create some of this information – punctuation, underlining, the use of different typefaces in printing – but most is lost. No wonder then that, with this handicap, writing is a difficult medium to master and 'written-down speech' an impossibility.

Writing has another handicap: it is a relatively slow, laborious process. Most people can speak at rates up to three words a second without undue difficulty. Writing longhand, the rate would be one-tenth of that. The invention of shorthand enabled speech to be captured verbatim, but with a time-and-effort penalty: the ultimate need to read back and transcribe.

Many of these differences may be expressed as oppositions, with the advantage going now to one mode, now to the other. Speech is transient; writing permanent. Speech is immediate; writing premeditated. The writer's audience may be known or unknown, near-at-hand or distant; the speaker (excluding the special cases of radio, television, telephone, record, tape) has his auditors face-to-face. Speech has to be edited, amended, restated in full flow, while writing may be reworked again and again before it reaches an audience.

The general implications of this analysis for teaching are plain enough. If speaking and writing are distinct modes, each with its own strengths and weaknesses and its own range of functions, these need to be acknowledged in what children are asked to do. In earlier school rooms, writing tended to be an inevitable part of every lesson, appropriate or not. Though the time has not yet come, the pendulum of practice might as easily swing the other way, with the tape-recorder replacing the exercise-book.

There is still more to a consideration of speaking and writing than this, arising from the very nature of language itself and how it relates to thinking and communicating. A speaker or writer does *not* begin with a message or an experience which he then encodes in language as a means of sending it to his hearer/reader. Speaking and writing are acts of creation. E. M. Forster was one of many writers who commented on the significance of the process : 'How can I know what I think until I see what I say?' Until we speak or write, our recognitions and perceptions of experience are unformed, inexplicit. Once written or spoken, they become shared property, related to the social systems of thinking, feeling and understanding that language itself expresses.

The force of this naturally enough varies according to the situation and the purpose for which language is being used. 'Two pints today, please' as a note to your milkman is in effect a formula, which comes ready-made from a large set of similar occurrences. The same is true of what the anthropologist, Malinowski, called 'phatic communion' : the use of language not to communicate or seek information, to give commands, to express hopes, wishes or desires, but to establish a bond between speaker and hearer, to fill a silence. Many of these exchanges are formulae, socially prescribed for particular contexts : 'How do you do?', 'Good morning', 'Nice day'. 'Pleased to meet you'. Beyond these opening moves in the language game, however, speaking becomes a creative process, a series of experiments in conveying shades of meaning, attitudes, beliefs, understandings, even in these polite exchanges between strangers.

This fundamental characteristic of the way human beings use language is obvious enough if we are alerted to listen for it or to discern its operation in print and writing. With exceptions of the kind just illustrated, speaking and writing are searches for meaning. This cannot be known until it is discovered, when the language is produced and its effect on the intended audience noted and interpreted. Yet in schools, we sometimes seem to proceed as though the reverse were true : the discovery being made, language is produced like a net to hold it. Children are filled to the brim with information, told, or advised, which pieces to choose, their order and emphasis, even the form the writing is to take. It is little wonder in these circumstances that personal discoveries of meaning are rare; the search for it has never been allowed to begin.

Two pieces of writing will illustrate the argument. First Michael, a bright, curious ten-year-old, writing to a 'formula' about his visit to York :

'I thought the most interesting thing at York was Kirk Gate. The shops seemed to be very well equipped indeed. The materials used were in excellent condition. I personally thought that the hansom-cab looked splendid with the surroundings. The sweet shop was well equipped, with a sweet-making machine and lots of sweets. The dresses in the dress shop looked excellent on the models. The brass models in the brass shop looked as though the things were modern made. The agricultural gallery had farming gear used in Yorkshire at the time of when they used horses. There were heavy wooden ploughs, stone rollers, seed drills, sithes, sickles and reapers. It is an interesting place.'

Next, Wendy, nine years old, with the same sort of verbal intelligence rating as Michael, on a similar trip. Here, though the children were prepared for the visit and encouraged to make notes on their observation and impressions (as were Michael's class), the writing was not tightly prescribed :

'On Wednesday June 9th we went on a trip to Stapleford Park. We set off at about 9 o'clock. The rain poured down and it was very cold. The sky was covered in threatening black clouds. Mr D stood at the gate with his umbrella wishing us a good time. "Some hope!" (I said to myself). The journey was long and boring and I soon began to feel sick. When I looked out of the window all there was to see was a bedraggled dog scrounging food and the pattering raindrops running down the glass. I decided to try and go to sleep. Everybody was under the impression that I was sleeping and I giggled quietly to myself. Afterwards I decided it was a foolish thing to join in the gossip and try to be merry. We sang, much against my will, until we arrived at the Park. Mrs J's class were going round the Lion Reserve with our class. I liked it when the lions went onto a mound and began to roar loudly as if trying to win a roaring competition. I breathed a sigh of relief when we at last arrived back at the stop for it had taken up most of our time. We were then allowed to have lunch. I had cheese sandwiches and a nasty shock – the cheese was mouldy. With a few lesser mishaps I finished my lunch and went to the souvenir shop I queued up for half an hour for nothing. I felt like going up to the front and demanding to be served at once. We went to Animal Land. Everywhere was muddy. The animals were lovely. I was scared that if I stood in one place long enough I would be stuck there. I liked the pumas, vulture, rabbits and skunk best for no reason at all because I really liked every one of the animals. Again I ended up with sweet nothing at the shop. The journey home was spent singing until we saw the church at Threekingham with the jaw bone of a whale. The rain had nearly stopped as the bus pulled up beside the gate for all the excitement of the Lion Reserve I could not really and truthfully say I had enjoyed it.'

Even allowing for the fact that Wendy is a much more enthusiastic writer than Michael normally, the differences are startling. Michael dutifully and accurately performs the exercise he was set. Wendy explores as she is writing the flavour and significance of the experience for her and provides her solemn judgement in the final sentence. For Michael the audience is the teacher; the objective, to meet a strictly limited set of expectations. Wendy is writing for the teacher too, but this is firmly subordinate to her primary purpose of writing for and to herself. Michael, in his circumstances, can only offer a half-hearted response. What purpose is there in describing the general features of an experience to an adult who saw them all for herself at the same time anyway? Wendy's response is uniquely hers; no one was standing in exactly the same spot and she realises the significance of this in providing a purpose for her writing.

Other themes arise in relation to these two pieces of writing and the contexts in which they emerged: the personal–impersonal dimension of response in writing, the search for ways to describe how children meet the challenge of a writing task, the language resources employed, the task of the teacher when the writing has appeared. These are considered in greater detail in the chapters which follow. For the moment, Michael's and Wendy's pieces stand as reminders of the need for purpose in writing, for sense of audience, for awareness of the expectations children recognise in their teachers.

To reiterate briefly the two main arguments of this chapter:

(1) before writing is undertaken it needs to be justified as an inescapable product of the experience that has preceded it. If speech or painting or model-making or silence are more appropriate, then they should occur. To treat writing as inevitably the most valuable outcome of learning is to diminish its unique properties.

(2) with relatively unimportant exceptions, writing is exploration of experience – the experience and the comprehending of it are in a real sense created by the words in which they are expressed. The way in which this is true may vary from personal to impersonal writing, but the underlying principle remains unaltered.

'Writing is fun when you know why.'

(John, aged 7½)

3

Varieties of Writing

'For a speech is composed of three things: the speaker, the subject on which he speaks and the audience he is addressing.'
(Aristotle – *Rhetoric*, Book 1)

'The student who writes or speaks to only one addressee, the same old teacher, cannot very well learn how to communicate in the range of situations that life presents.'
(James Moffett – *Teaching the Universe of Discourse*)

At the end of the last chapter, the pieces of writing from Michael and Wendy were used as examples in an attempt to establish the importance of having a fully-understood purpose in writing; a purpose which would bear close examination. This may seem too trite an observation to merit any further consideration or, if further elaborated, a reflection on the professional competence of teachers in this area of their activities. The elaboration which follows is aimed at demonstrating that neither assumption is warranted.

To begin with Aristotle on the elements of a speech might appear to be a strangely capricious choice, but the concerns of the orator became increasingly, with the passage of time, the concerns of the writer. The Greek analysis of the art of rhetoric, extended and refined by, among others, Cicero and Quintilian in Roman times, not only exerted a pervasive influence on Western European literature well into the modern era, but also shaped attitudes to the balance and emphasis of school curricula. Rhetoric was one of the three liberal arts (with grammar and logic) which formed the trivium, the opening sections of the curriculum in medieval and Renaissance schools. Accordingly the categories, classifications and rules of rhetorical theory became a universal currency in dealing with speaking and writing.

The orator's was, in origin at least, a strictly practical art and the divisions and rules of rhetoric reflected this closely. Three types of discourse were recognised:

(1) *forensic* (or judicial), where the concern was with a past event and the purpose the discovery of truth and the administration of justice;
(2) *deliberative*, which examined possible future events with the aim of determining right courses of action;
(3) *demonstrative*, concerned with the qualities of people, with the purpose of praising the virtuous and censuring the vicious.

This classification of kinds of oration (and later, by extension, kinds of writing) has a two-fold basis in relation to Aristotle's three elements. It takes account of subject matter *and* of audience and the rhetoricians prescribed appropriate styles of prose for each of the three kinds: ethical, emotional and precisely controlled respectively. Their *functions*, though, were identical: to present arguments so as to persuade the given audience to adopt the speaker/writer's point of view.

As a complete and satisfying method of describing varieties of discourse this is obviously defective; not surprisingly, since its purpose was deliberately limited to a set of practical situations. It does, though, point to the complexities involved in producing such a description, by drawing attention to the necessary ingredients. At one level these are writer, subject, audience, taken singly and (as the rhetoric example demonstrates) in interactions with each other. The fourth element, purpose or function, is derived from the interplay of these three. Even these do not exhaust the possible bases for a classification of writing varieties. Form is one important criterion: the shape and extent of a piece. The essay-composition distinction, with its attendant problems, discussed in Chapter 2, is one clear example. More universal still is the difference we assert between prose and poetry, each accompanied by further and finer sub-divisions: short story, novella, novel; sonnet, ode, ballad, *haiku*. Another method, less obvious but with relevance in teaching and learning, is to use the nature of the writing task as the focus. Is it given or imposed by some outside agency, or freely self-chosen? Is it undertaken to test a skill (an exercise) or to satisfy some more distant end?

By permuting and combining all these elements an almost endless series of writing classifications would be possible. Many exist, for reasons related to the uses they are put to. What is important here is to decide which is of greatest value in teaching; indeed to justify a concern for being able to describe writing in this way in the first place. At the same time, it must be admitted that the search for a perfect system is bound to fail. Writing will refuse to fit into a cut and dried scheme of labels, no matter how cunningly or patiently constructed. We are all aware, as readers, of this refusal and of attempts to coin new labels to bring the system back to neatness and harmony: free verse, concrete poetry, documentary novel, creative biography. No perfect system then, but one with the fewest disadvantages for the teacher's needs is the object of the search.

CLASSIFICATION SYSTEMS

(1) By *content, subject matter*. The most straightforward and widespread method is undoubtedly the one which sets out to answer, of any piece of writing, 'What is it about?' All library systems are essentially of this kind because this question is answered by the reader's needs. In the Dewey decimal system he looks for books about mathematics on shelves labelled 510–19. With sharply-focused adult writing such a system works well, though many books pose formidable problems of classification for highly skilled library staff. Work by children presents added complications. Daisy Ashford's *The Young Visiters*, though the work of a nine-year-old, is usually granted the status of novel, classified 823 and shelved with fiction (though often in the junior section of a library). An anthology of children's imaginative writing might be similarly treated, though it is far more likely to appear under 'Education' with the label 372.5 and has been seen as 808.1 (the art of writing).

Attempts have been made to devise simplified 'content' classifications for teaching purposes. One outlined by J. C. Nesfield in his *Manual of English Grammar and Composition*s will stand as representative of these:

technical — the concern of the specialist; purpose-instruction;
non-technical — for a general audience; purpose may include instruction but it also seeks to entertain. Its sub-divisions: history, biography, description, reflection, fiction, persuasion, censure, humour.

It will immediately be clear that this is only superficially a content classification: it includes, apparently unavoidably, reference to audience and purpose.

Wendy's account of her experience in the nature reserve is a puzzle for users of these systems because it refuses to be neatly pinned down. It is autobiography, reflection, description, humour, all at the same time.
(2) By *form*. Reference has already been made to some of the common categories here: prose/poetry; essay/composition. For special purposes, terms have been devised which can be placed in roughly hierarchical form. In scientific research such a sequence might be: note, article, report, monograph with dissertation and thesis as related categories.

For general use, classifying by form would rarely be precise enough by itself; something of content or audience would need to be added. No great advance is made by labelling Wendy's writing as prose rather than poetry, or as composition rather than essay.

(3) By *audience*. Rhetorical theory recognised a distinction between learned and popular audiences and the question 'Who am I writing for?' is a critically important one for the writer to consider. This system is, however, more profitably linked with its natural extensions.

(4) By *writer-audience relationship*. The Dutch linguist, Martin Joos, in his book *The Five Clocks*, entertainingly analyses the ways in which every speaker adjusts his language to the variety of situations in which he employs it. His 'five clocks' are the five major styles of language among which we choose and, though he is primarily concerned with accounting for speech events, the styles apply to writing too :

Style	Audience	Typical Language Features
frozen	universal	compression, explicitness
formal	strangers (passive)	elaboration, absence of writer reference
consultative	strangers (active)	1st person reference, direct address to audience
casual	friends, acquaintances	ellipsis, slang
intimate	those closely, permanently related	jargon, extreme selection

Letter writing affords an illustration of how some of these styles are marked by particular conventions. The sequence 'Dear Sir', 'Dear Mr Hawkins', 'Dear Jim' is related to the formal, consultative and casual styles we would expect in the letters following such salutations. The correspondence is not exact; letters to editors conventionally begin 'Sir' but may adopt any one of the three styles according to the presumed audience.

When this classification is tried out on Wendy's writing, its informative potential becomes clear. Her key style is consultative, but she slips effortlessly into casual and formal when her purpose demands it. Michael, in contrast, operates uneasily and stiltedly in formal style throughout.

Another way of looking at speaker-audience connections is used by James Moffett (*Teaching the Universe of Discourse*). He concentrates attention on the identity of the participants and on the distance between them, arriving at a four-fold classification :

reflection	– where speaker and listener are identical; a communication between two parts of one nervous system;
conversation	– interpersonal communication between two people in vocal range of each other;
correspondence	– communication between remote individuals or small groups with some knowledge of each other;
publication	– impersonal communication to a large anonymous group extended over space and/or time.

The virtue of this system is in its first term; it allows us to account for *private* language, written and spoken. Talking to oneself (aloud or silently), notes to aid memory, writing aimed solely at clarifying an idea or aiding an understanding, all belong to *reflection*. Again to use Wendy's writing as a test of the system, her choice fluctuates among the first three categories, though, because of the different emphasis in this classification method, the dominant mode is perhaps reflection where one might expect conversation from the analysis in terms of the Joos categories.

One further method needs to be treated under this heading, though its concerns go somewhat beyond writer and audience. This is the notion of *register*. The term has gained wide currency in language study over the past decade, though still much argued over, and it has particular relevance in school because of its stress on the idea of appropriateness in language.

Borrowing the formulation of Geoffrey Leech (*A Linguistic Guide to English Poetry*), register is defined as 'the language a writer is prompted to use by the situation he is in'. There are three elements :

medium	– speech, writing;
tone	– determined by the social relation between participants and leading to distinctions such as colloquial/formal, familiar/polite, personal/ impersonal;
rôle	– the place of language in those human activities and institutions connected with the communication.

The last of these is the new dimension. Michael, writing for his teacher, in school, with a recognisably 'educational' task, adopts the register of what might be called 'school' language, based on what he believes are the expectations of him in these circumstances. This is a version of the language of textbooks, of exercises, of the teacher's conscious or unconscious models. Wendy creates a register of her own, flexible yet still meeting with ease the requirements of the task she is facing.

(5) By *writer and task*. This is of considerable importance since it has in many ways become a dominant system in schools. As 'composition' became a taboo word, so the need for a replacement descriptive term made itself felt. With the notion of 'audience' in the closed classroom situations considered to be of little relevance, the emphasis, perhaps naturally, fell on the writer and what he was being asked to accomplish. Those terms from the fifties and sixties discussed in Chapter 2 fall comfortably into this category: creative, free, intensive, imaginative, personal for one kind of view of experience; practical, factual, recording, 'topic' for another. 'Audience' was not entirely overlooked, since many exponents of creative writing stressed that the writer worked to express his meanings to himself and reinforced this by arguing that such work was not intended for assessment, marking or appraisal in the normal school way. Though some of these labels were initially used with precision and effect, 'creative', in particular, has now almost reached the point of sharing the fate of 'composition': a prescription for a narrow orthodoxy, with purpose in writing almost lost sight of.

As classification systems, their shortcomings are obvious. Wendy's piece was, in origin, 'factual', but it would be hard to deny that it is in the full sense 'creative' too.

(6) By *function, purpose, intention*. For the classical rhetorician, the purpose of public speaking was strictly practical; to argue a case, to persuade a court, a legislative assembly or a public gathering to take a course of action or to adopt a set of attitudes and beliefs. When the emphasis moves from speech to writing, other purposes become important, though it can be argued that persuasion, in some form, is present in every communication. J. A. K. Thomson in *Classical Influences on English Prose* added narration to persuasion and produced a two-category system:

narration – legend, anecdote, short story, history, biography, romance, novel;
persuasion – oratory, philosophy, science.

This left out of account some awkward kinds of writing: satire, letters, travel, 'characters', which he treated separately.

Herbert Read and Bonamy Dobrée, in explaining the shape of their anthology, *The London Book of English Prose*, defined three major functions for writing as:

(1) to tell a story   – in which category they include letters and 'characters' as well as Thomson's set;

(2) to describe a thing — natural sciences, philosophy, theology, politics, law, tactics, sport, criticism;

(3) to produce an emotional effect— pathos, drama, oratory, comedy, satire, controversy, moralistic writing.

They add, understandably enough, a cautionary rider: few pieces of writing are single in their aim. Even scientific discourse, concerned with observation and inference, can concern itself with more than description and intellectual persuasion. Faraday, for instance, on the 'chemical history of a candle':

'You observe a candle is a very different thing from a lamp. With a lamp you take a little oil, fill your vessel, put in a little moss or some cotton prepared by artificial means, and then light the top of the wick. When the flame runs down the cotton to the oil, it gets extinguished, but it goes on burning in the part above. Now I have no doubts you will ask, how is it that the oil, which will not burn itself, gets up to the top of the cotton, where it will burn? . . . but there is a much more wonderful thing about the burning of a candle than this. You have here a solid substance with no vessel to contain it; and how is it that this solid substance can get up to the place where the flame is? How is it that this solid gets there, it not being a fluid? or, when it is made a fluid, then how is it that it keeps together? This is a wonderful thing about a candle.' (from Lecture 1 of a series of six, 1849)

H. J. C. Grierson (in *Rhetoric and English Composition*) also offers a three-fold purpose classification, but with a significant variation from the preceding:

(1) to convey information;
(2) to induce others to act in a certain way;
(3) to give pleasure, to interest and delight by wit, feeling or imagination.

These he relates closely to a general subject classifying system:

(1) the order of phenomena in space: the relative position of co-existing things – all *descriptive* writing;
(2) the order of phenomena in time – all *historical* writing whether real or fictitious;
(3) the order of thoughts in the mind: the logical dependence of one truth on another – all *expository* writing.

One final example of classifying writing by function is necessary to conclude this account of methods and the complexities inherent in devising them. Professor James Britton and his associates, in the course of an enquiry into the written language of 11–18-year-olds in schools, were faced with the need to differentiate kinds of writing among the many hundred pieces drawn from the major subject areas. They rejected the traditional 'function' approach for its practical shortcomings, some of which have been discussed in this section. If we use the writer's intention as a guide, we have to guess whether the intentions we see in the writing correspond to the writer's own. If effect on audience is the criterion, we must make the unwarranted assumption that all readers will necessarily be affected as we are. For intention and effect defined in these ways, Britton substitutes function *signalled by choices in the language used*. If we meet a piece of writing which begins 'Once upon a time', past experience tells us that this is a selection from the repertoire of fictional narrative and we know what kind of writing should follow.

Changing the evidence for classification in this way has repercussions on the structure of the system. Categories are no longer separate, but represent positions on a single continuum:

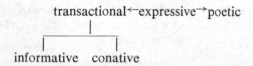

As its central position indicates, the expressive is seen as the fundamental language function, out of which the others emerge as the needs of writer/speaker and audience change. What are its characteristics?

Expressive speech or writing has 'I' at the centre. It relies very considerably on a shared situation with its intended audience; to understand it fully the listener/reader must be part of the situation, because much of the meaning is implicit. To return to Moffett's labels (p. 39), most of reflection and conversation belongs here. In writing notes, thinking on paper, many diary entries, some personal letters, are expressive. Some apparently more public writing can assume expressive characteristics too, when the distance between writer and reader is deliberately reduced: gossip columns in newspapers, informally 'conversational' autobiographies are instances of this.

With transactional writing, both informative and conative, we are back on familiar ground. Here conveying information and persuading others are the major variants for using language to get things done.

Recording facts, describing events, expressing opinions, explaining ideas, constructing theories, offering advice, regulating the behaviour of others, all conform to this definition.

In this scheme, further sub-divisions are suggested for both the informative and conative categories. For *informative* these are:

record	– what is happening? : the eye-witness account;
report	– what happened? : narratives in past tense;
generalised narrative/ description	– both what happened? and what happens? : this would include, among other things, the writing in practical handbooks (e.g. recipes);
analogic (first level of generalisation)/ true analogic	– what happens? : as the subject extends and the writer gets further from the phenomena he is concerned with, classification becomes a key element. Much scientific writing is of this kind;
speculative	– what may happen? writing where generalisations are examined to form a basis for prediction;
tautologic	– a disciplined, highly ordered form of the speculative: theoretical science, logic, metaphysics.

Conative writing has two aspects. The first is *persuasion*, which figures so largely in the rhetorical system. The other is *regulation*, where writing is used directly to control behaviour. The Ten Commandments, by-laws, school rules, all signal their function in language: imperatives, negation, direction, often the impersonal ('It is forbidden to . . .').

Poetic writing is its own justification: an object made out of language to please the writer. For the reader, the invitation is to share that pleasure and to hold back reference to his own experience until he has grasped what the text is offering. Poetic writing may invite a secondary label from elsewhere in the system: *Animal Farm* as poetic-persuasive; *Catcher in the Rye* as poetic-expressive; *Robinson Crusoe* as poetic-informative. What is important in identifying this function is to determine whether the writing exists in and for itself or as a means to some end. An election speech in blank verse or purple prose is still transactional, in spite of the language signals.

(Note: more extensive discussions of this system will be found in the works listed in the Bibliography by Britton and Burgess.)

THE USE OF CLASSIFICATIONS IN TEACHING

The connection between these elaborate systems and the job of helping children to write may well seem tenuous, particularly for the young children, the beginning writers we are concerned with. These are ways of describing the full range of mature, adult writing, seen from any one of a number of standpoints; a world away from the first efforts of the learner. Yet there are at least three good reasons for arguing that they have great significance for the teacher:

(1) They offer an aiming point, an ideal view of the end of the process we are engaged in. To teach writing at any stage is to contribute to a child's chance of ultimately mastering as much of the world of writing as he can grasp, both as writer and reader. Evidence from the writing research suggested that teachers, concentrating hard on providing situations for writing, could lose sight of the need to extend the range of writing kinds (of which more in Chapter 5).
(2) They draw attention very powerfully to the significant features in the circumstances of writing and especially to the writer's situation, his audience and his purpose. They provide warrant for a summarising proposition about writing: it should come *from* experience, *for* an audience, *with* a purpose.
(3) They suggest new and potentially fruitful ways of talking to children about their writing to add to those we use already (selection of subject matter, control of language, evaluation of overall effect). Two at least of those outlined (Moffett, Britton) have the added advantage of providing a structure for a developmental programme in writing.

If these arguments are accepted, two tasks remain. The first is choice of system, in the light of the earlier admission that no scheme of categories will answer all questions about kinds of writing. In the circumstances of learning and teaching, the chief elements to emerge concern awareness of audience and purpose, in order to exorcise those demons of past practice, the exercise (restriction of purpose) and the teacher-reader (restriction of audience). Writer-audience and functional systems are obvious candidates for the job and they gain in effectiveness by operating together. For instance the Moffett categories point to a development from concern with 'I' through 'I-you' to 'I-it'; in each of these positions a choice of functions is open and entry to a system like Britton's shows the range of possibilities available. They complement each other in another way too. 'Reflection', 'conversation', 'correspondence', 'publication' express differences in writer-audience space; 'transactional' and 'poetic' develop in time from the 'expressive' beginnings.

The second task is to descend from these theoretical justifications in an attempt to discover the utility of these descriptions for the writer-as-learner and for his teacher to bring them to life in children's writing.

It will be obvious that the progression from expressive writing to either poetic or the varieties of transactional does not take place as the result of a single, blinding flash of understanding. From the expressive base we move through an indeterminate number of transitional experiments; trying out other voices, other standpoints, other purposes until we feel secure in meeting the writing demands of categories such as persuasive or analogic. No account exists of these transitional stages, though most teachers will have an intuitive awareness of them and of the occasions when they attract often critical attention. After a history lesson on the Stone Age an eleven-year-old was set to 'write about life' in the period. His writing took the form of narrative, a tale of hunter and hunted, which carried, in fictional form, much of the information from the lesson. The comment was 'a good story – but not much history'. This teacher, expecting a transactional (report) piece, rejected expressive→poetic writing as inappropriate though the vagueness of his instructions made either response possible. (I am indebted to Colin Harrison for this example.)

Some examples from the writing of the 'project' children will show the variety and movement in these transitional areas. First, two first-year juniors (7·9 years old) reacting to a simple experiment:

(John) 'We got a candle and lit it than we got a Jam Jar full of water and put the crystals in the Jam Jar and than we put the Jam Jar over the candle and we watched we found that the crystals flowed up becuse het rises and if the het rises it takes the crystals up.'

(Kevin) 'When I put some crystals in a Jam Jar They sunk but when I put it on the candle the crystals wat up to the top of the Jam Jar it was because heat travels throw the Jar to get to the top of the ceiling.'

Both boys are working out of expressive towards transactional. John's more inclusive personal pronoun suggests he is further on the road, but both attempt to go beyond the description of incident: they try to account for what they saw. Kevin's inference is tightly tied to that particular time and place; it is the heat on *that* jam jar. John momentarily is concerned with the general effects of heat before returning to the behaviour of the crystals. They are both still a country mile from the impersonal report ('It was observed that, when heat was applied to the container . . .'), further still from impersonal generalisation ('When heat is applied to water, convection currents are set up which . . .'), but they are on their way. In Moffett's terms, Kevin has decided on 'conversation', John on 'correspondence'.

The pleasurable recall of experience, the satisfaction we get from sharing this with others, is central to the expressive mode of speaking and writing. James Britton, following and extending an idea of D. W. Harding's, uses the term 'gossip' for the varieties of this activity. As it moves towards external ends, gossip becomes transactional. Moving the other way, the emphasis falls increasingly on the form of the discourse, where no practical outcomes are aimed at. This is the domain of the poetic mode, of literature; for, as Auden has it, 'poetry makes nothing happen'. For our young writers, a kind of autobiographical gossip is a dominating choice in their work. A piece by 9-year-old Lynn will stand as representative of this unshaped reliving of experience, which all teachers will instantly recognise :

'Last night I went to the Fair. I won a cocanut. The man at the cocanut shy was a jolly old man he let me have a free go. Netch I went to the big wheel and had a lovely ride you could see over the city and the lights of the fair looked butfull. I had a ride on the roundabout it went very fast. I went to get a candey flouse it was a very big one then I had a ride on a rooket when I came off it i felt dizzy so I went and sat down then I went and got a drink. When i felt better i went and had a few more rides and then I went home i was happy tired.'

Just how children are influenced in exploring routes out of the expressive is not a matter for confident assertions, but the shaping power of stories often seems to be at work. In the following piece, Steven, a 10-year-old, retains the autobiographical 'I', but moves himself in time and space :

'On the night of January 30th 1739, Dick Turpin was brought to our cell. He called himself John Palmer. He wrote a letter to his brother but he denied the handwriting saying it was not John Palmer's handwriting. Luck was not with Turpin for his schoolmaster recognised the handwriting. He told me and with some other warders we brought him to our prison. By now the date was March 31st. We put him in our condemned cell. He was to die. But not for being a highwayman, but for stealing horses. The cell was gloomy and dark. The bed was an iron frame with no covers or anything. It was a hard frame. It must have been very hard to go to sleep on it expecially as rats were running all over the floor. It was hopeless to escape because the window is about $4\frac{1}{2}$ yards off the ground. The roll of drums has started and we are marching Dick Turpin to the gallows. He is now on our cart. The noose is round his neck. Instead of dying normally, he jumped from the cart. That was the end of Dick Turpin FOR GOOD!'

The signs of inexperience are plain enough: slight confusions in the order of events, a struggle with the subtleties of tense. Yet the reaching out towards the poetic is vouched for by the form the narrative is given.

A more concrete instance of shaping is demonstrated in the final example. Here Gina, another 10-year-old, tries to catch the pattern and movement of experience on the page as well as in the words. After hearing a reading of Frances Cornford's poem 'Mornings at the Hall', her group had been talking about morning and waking up. The 'I' of this piece is more detached, more contemplative than in Lynn's and Steven's narratives.

'The dawn is here, a call of a cock tells me that,
Everything is still, but then the clock strikes five.
The peace carries on for an hour, but after that the early birds start off,
　In cars and motor bikes
　I know the peace is broken.

I see a little old lady, a bus, she is probably going to catch.
Some lights go on. The clock strikes seven.
The curtains are drawn, Weary people trudge around the house
People come out with their dogs taking them before they go to work
　I know the peace is broken.

Then comes eight. Children come out of their houses,
The children's patrol men came out with their red warning signs.
　Then comes nine.
Ten brings the women and prams, to do the daily shopping
Eleven comes, and then comes twelve,
　Morning's gone.'

There would be no difficulty in extending indefinitely this selection of illustrations to show the great range of experiments children make in venturing out of the expressive centre. The significance of these explorations for teaching are examined in more detail in Chapter 6.

The examples, with the interleaving comments, are intended to show just how a category system can offer a new way of looking at children's writing, to reinforce those we customarily employ. Function and audience, as a result, occupy the central position in our attention that they deserve and need.

Readers interested in other examples of what might now be called 'functional analysis' should find Chapters 2 and 3 of *Understanding Children Writing* (by Tony Burgess and others) illuminating. There the range of examples includes work from secondary school pupils.

One cautionary epilogue is worth setting down. A scheme of categories, a system of classifications, is a diagnostic tool, not a set of models for prescription. Categories like these help us to understand the variety of purposes in writing so that we can encourage our pupils to develop them. They also alert us to the complex blend of motives and intentions in what we say or write. They cannot be used as simple measuring rods, as 'a good story, but not much history' testifies. That way takes us back to the rigidity of old-style 'composition' and writing as an artificial exercise.

4
Language and Writing Development

'With the exception of lexical refinement, the organisation of syntax appears to be complete in most respects by four or five.'
(D. McNeill – *The Acquisition of Language*)

'The second stage of learning the native language is learning the grammatical system . . . it is complete and the books are closed on it! – at about eight years of age. It is not normal to learn any more grammar beyond that age.'
(Martin Joos – *Language Arts in the Elementary School*)

'Recent language research has given rise to the suspicion that the child of five or six may still not have mastered certain – perhaps surprisingly many – aspects of the structure of his language that the mature speaker takes for granted and commands quite naturally.'
(Carol Chomsky – *The Acquisition of Syntax in Children from 5 to 10*)

Children progress in their uniquely individual ways, at their own speeds, in mastering first the physical skill of writing and then in exploring its potentialities. The manner of the exploration, its rapidity and extent, clearly depend on a host of circumstances, physical, psychological, social, environmental. Some of these influences are considered later in this chapter and elsewhere, though it is as well to recognise that those we are able to define and describe are only a small part of a very complex whole. For all the individual variations that children show in this progress, there are some underlying, fundamental features which seem to permit an attempt to construct a developmental sequence, however cautiously phrased. There is an order to the development, even though our perception of it is still very imperfect. But this development rests crucially on another: the acquisition of language.

Before writing there is speech, and speech itself is only one outward sign of the process of learning language. How language mastery develops is a question inseparable from progress in writing, even though its ramifications spread well beyond the immediate scope of this book. The quotations at the head of this chapter give some indication that in this area, as in so many with which we are concerned, disagreements and uncertainties are not hard to find. Some of these problems may be more apparent than real: what writer A means by 'organisation of syntax' may not be equivalent to writer B's 'grammatical system'.

One method of testing hypotheses about the extent to which language had been mastered is to use an adult speaker or writer as a measure. William Boyd reported in 1927 on an experiment using his daughter to provide the language evidence. From the age of 2 up to age 9, he collected 1,250 unselected sentences around the time of her birthday each year. After studying this material in detail he concluded that by age 8, the speech of children approaches very closely the adult form: he claimed that of the 1,250 sentences for that year, only 50 betrayed their origin. Reservations are not difficult to find. He generalises from a particular child to most children, but this was the child of a highly intelligent man, whose powerful interest in language was likely to have had a profound effect on the linguistic environment in which his child grew up. The circumstances in which the talk occurred are of crucial importance, as we have seen earlier, particularly in relation to the audience addressed, but Boyd says nothing of this. Again which adult standard? It could be Boyd himself, or written 'conversation' (he analyses 100 sentences from each of eighteen authors to provide a comparative standard) or some generalised expectations of how adults customarily speak.

These examples counsel caution in attempting wide-ranging generalisations on stages in language mastery. It is enough, perhaps, to agree that by the time children reach school they are already expert speakers and listeners in a wide range of situations, though their experience will be strongly affected by variations in circumstances. They possess the core of language resources, but much remains to be discovered of their flexibility, power and usefulness. Writing and reading, as new language skills, have to be deliberately learnt and assimilated to existing understanding.

The use of a term like 'resources' raises another important consideration. Language works very obviously through metaphor, reinforced by our ways of representing experience in language. In English we recognise a distinction between elements in a process and the process itself, with the elements represented by nouns or their equivalents and the process by verbs. So to talk of language 'resources' is to invite the image of countable things, held in store, ready for use. Our Saxon ancestors made this picture more immediately vivid by describing the act of speaking as 'unlocking the word-hoard'. A recent writer (Peter Doughty in *Exploring Language*) employs the analogy of a Meccano set where the pieces represent elements of a language. Metaphors and analogies in the case we are considering may be both useful and misleading, particularly when they shape practices in learning and teaching.

The danger is that the metaphor or the analogy takes over. If there is a store of words, it is a short step to statements of quantity: more, less, rich, impoverished. With the idea of a deficit established, providing additional material is an apparently logical consequence. Much of the vocabulary work in schools is a direct response to this persuasive reasoning, but it misses the over-simplification inherent in metaphor and analogy. The likeness is *only* partial. Language is process and behaviour; its elements have no independent existence. Words and structures have meaning only in use.

DESCRIBING THE LANGUAGE OF WRITING

When children begin the process of learning to write there is a big gap between their general language competence and their performance. The effort involved in learning the new skill is considerable and attention is, naturally enough, on the mechanics of the business. What is drawn on from those oral language resources is sharply restricted. As the act of writing becomes habitual, so more opportunity is available to bring oral competence and written performance into harmony, with the proviso, noted earlier, that these are two distinct modes. The writing beginner *looks* like a language beginner, but clearly is not.

The Russian psychologist, Lev Vygotsky, investigating the ways in which children develop intellectually, explained very clearly the problems of the transition from speaking to writing (in Chapter 6 of his book *Thought and Language*):

'Written speech is a separate linguistic function, differing from oral speech in both structure and mode of functioning. Even its minimal development requires a high level of abstraction ... In learning to write, the child must disengage himself from the sensory aspect of speech and replace words by images of words ... Our studies show that it is the abstract quality of written language that is the main stumbling block, not the underdevelopment of small muscles or any other mechanical obstacles. Writing is also speech without an interlocutor, addressed to an absent or imaginary person or to no one in particular – a situation new and strange to the child . . . In written speech we are obliged to create the situation, to represent it to ourselves. This demands detachment from the actual situation . . . The discrepancy between competence in speaking and writing is caused by the child's proficiency in spontaneous, unconscious activity and his lack of skill in abstract, deliberate activity . . . Grammar and writing help the child to rise to a higher level of speech development.'

Though Vygotsky is less inclined to accept the physical difficulty of making marks on paper as an important consideration in learning to write, there is a high measure of agreement with the analysis suggested earlier, but with one significant addition: the practice of writing extends the mastery of speech. If this is true, and Vygotsky argues persuasively for it, another very powerful justification for writing is created to reinforce those already advanced.

In order to explain and discuss what happens when children write and to account for changes over a period of time, we need to produce a method for systematically describing the writing itself. Again, as in the case of providing categories for kinds of writing, the choice of methods is bewilderingly wide. Which ones are selected will depend to some extent on the reasons for employing them at all, but more important is a consideration of their respective strengths and weaknesses. There is no single perfect system.

Word Count

When the 290 children in our experiment had produced four pieces of writing a term over the six terms' period in which we followed their progress, we possessed nearly 7,000 pieces in all, amounting to a little under 800,000 words in total. Nothing easier, with all the figures available, to calculate the average length of a piece from our pupils, but what use would such an average be? So many influences are at work in shaping how much writing is done: the topic, the time available, the known expectations of the teacher, even the kind of writing instrument and the size of paper.

The argument for such an average, as a measure of fluency, is that over a number of writing assignments a characteristic pattern of response by individual children is likely to emerge, particularly in these early stages of writing development. A similarity can be seen with judgements of children as 'talkative' or 'quiet'.

The table that follows should be read with these precautions in mind:

(1) comparisons should be made with several pieces of work, not with just one;

(2) a comparable average figure would need to be calculated from any two pieces from the middle of the first term and two from the third term in a year;
(3) as the table indicates, kind of writing must be matched;
(4) averages often conceal wide variations – two pieces of 390 and 10 words respectively yield the same figure as two of 200;
(5) girls can be expected to be about 10 per cent more productive than boys, e.g. for C writing in the second year, the boys' figure would be 114, the girls' 126.

For convenience, the kinds of writing described at the end of Chapter 1 are represented by abbreviations, both in this table and subsequently. 'Personal' or 'creative' writing is listed as C, with the addition of V to incorporate the full verbal preparation. 'Factual' or 'recording' writing appears similarly as F and FV.

Table 1   *Average length of writing in words*

Age group	C	CV	F	FV
1st year	91	127	58	77
2nd year	120	148	84	112
3rd year	158	170	105	122
4th year	172	210	123	143

The range in our collection is predictably wide. The shortest single piece was just 7 words, the longest in excess of 1,100. Total output of writing over the two years varied from under 500 words for one child to close on 8,000 at the other extreme.

One further point is worth making. Towards the end of their junior-school life, our fourth-year children were markedly reducing the rate of their advance in output of writing. With evidence from other parts of the analysis, this suggests a period of consolidation, when newly acquired skills are tested and more thoroughly mastered and, perhaps, the beginning of a concern for economy and selection in shaping what is written. For teachers, this indicates the opportunity to help pupils make this process more effective by discussion, the use of a wide range of examples and by shared experiments in obtaining desired effects.

Vocabulary
Teachers are familiar with investigations of vocabulary, from the informal level of assessing whether a word is understood in speaking,

writing or reading, to more formal applications in a variety of tests, notably those labelled 'verbal reasoning'.

Interest in the vocabulary of children has a long and distinguished history, with most emphasis falling on vocabulary growth in early childhood or on establishing frequencies of use of words at different ages. Tests of vocabulary range have been constructed, usually on the basis of a dictionary-sampling technique, and are widely used to assist in age-linked comparisons. 'She has a remarkable vocabulary for her age' or 'he has a very limited vocabulary' are judgements that need the support of a reliable test if they are to be anything more than hopeful assertions. Even the best test is, of course, a victim of the changes brought about by time. Words disappear from use, are sometimes reborn, take on new meanings, are created to meet new needs. 'Television' would have been a very rare word in the recognition vocabulary of children in the 1940s; in the 1970s it would be difficult to find a child of school age in this country who would not respond to it (or, more accurately to the word and its variants : 'telly', 'teevee').

The need to distinguish 'use' vocabularies in speaking and writing from recognition vocabularies led to enquiries into the frequency of appearance of words in speaking, writing and printing. These word lists are monuments to patient endeavour, usually by American scholars. Thorndike produced a word frequency list in 1921 and, in its 1931 revision, this contains 20,000 words. H. D. Rinsland collected writing by children from 708 schools, 200,000 pieces amounting to more than 6,000,000 words. His analysis of this enormous collection appeared in 1945 as *A Basic Vocabulary of Elementary School Children*, with the frequencies of the 25,000 different words carefully tabulated.

In Great Britain, vocabulary studies have tended to be linked with concerns in the teaching of reading, particularly in connection with the identification of what could be defined as a 'basic' reading vocabulary. Burroughs, in a typical survey, studied the speech vocabulary of 330 children aged 5–6½ and produced a frequency list based not on the number of occurrences of a word, but on the number of its users. His results showed 1,900 words used by five or more children in the group tested, with a further 1,600 used by four children or fewer. On the basis of a number of studies of this kind, both British and American, McNally and Murray arrived at what they believed to be a list of 'key' words, the foundation of a basic reading vocabulary. In its final form this list consisted of 200 words, accounting for some 65 per cent of vocabulary in common use. Since nouns were, not surprisingly, under-represented (only 21 in the 200), 50 commonly used nouns were added and a further 50 words frequently met with in early formal schooling. On the foundation of these 300 'Key Words to Literacy', the Ladybird reading series was devised.

Our enquiry did not touch directly on vocabulary for two reasons : the sheer size of the task when added to all the others; and its relative usefulness, bearing in mind all the influences affecting vocabulary choice. This should not be read as a judgement that a study of children's vocabulary is of little value, when the reverse is plainly true. In the end, it is a question of deciding which, among many possibilities, will be a useful and practicable exploration for teaching purposes. To relate the vocabulary range of English children in 1974 with their American counterparts of the 1940s may have some value, but this is a long way removed from a teacher's immediate concerns. What can we learn about vocabulary resources by studying a child's writing without reference to often-remote outside information?

One technique provides the beginnings of an answer to questions on range of vocabulary and its flexibility in use. If the number of different words (types) in a piece of writing is expressed as a proportion of the total number of words (tokens), a type-token ratio (TTR) emerges. The previous paragraph contains 135 words; of these 99 are different, giving a ratio of 0·73 or thereabouts. Because the TTR decreases with the length of the sample, stretches of speech or writing should be divided into equal segments, of 50 or 100 words, if comparisons are to be made. Earlier research suggests that, for children aged 7–11, ratios for the first 100 words tend to range in value from 0·45–0·70. The TTR is a reasonably sensitive measure of the diversity of vocabulary in use and is an important complement to results from recognition vocabulary tests. The sharper the drop in TTR after the first 100 words, the less diverse a child's vocabulary resources are likely to be.

Language Structures

A study of vocabulary concentrates on particular units of language, considered separately; it examines the occurrence of words, or more strictly lexical items, in stretches of speech and writing. As language users though, we are aware that words have distinct functions, and are grouped together to form identifiable patterns. When we pay attention to patterns and structures, our concern is for the *grammar* of the language we are dealing with.

The number of patterns and structures in the language we produce is very large indeed. To describe them all is to write a complete grammar of that language, something not yet achieved for any natural language. Making a selection of features for study is, then, essential, but which are likely to prove most significant in showing how children move towards mastery of their native language?

In print and writing, certain conventions direct us to major units of structure, notably *paragraph* (signalled by indentation) and *sentence* (with its opening capital letter and concluding full-stop). So little is known about the grammar of the paragraph that it makes sense to ignore it for the purposes of analysis. The idea of sentence, too, is not without its difficulties, particularly when the work of novice writers is under scrutiny; the punctuation of 8-year-olds is rarely a reflection of linguistic propriety. For our work, a supplementary definition was added, borrowed from the American linguist Leonard Bloomfield. For him a sentence was 'a linguistic form, not included by virtue of any grammatical construction in any larger linguistic form'. Even this does not solve all problems. Children use one grammatical construction with a freedom that teachers often equate with wild abandon – the conjunction 'and'. Thus, Mark: 'One day two boys went fishing and they had some jam-jars and they caught some stiklebats and they saw a mill and they explod it and one brother got lost.' One sentence or several? By punctuation and by definition, only one, but most adult readers would suggest dividing it into at least three sections; some, conservatively, would argue for six.

Other rules usually working in combination may be added in an attempt to deal with this uncertainty. Teachers who would like to use the figures, given later, for the purposes of comparison, should note the three that we implemented. These were to assume the need for a sentence division where

(1) three or more elements were conjoined – 'John walked into the forest and he met a fierce wolf and he ran away',
(2) the subject is repeated – '*they* went to the park and *they* walked round the lake',
(3) there is no immediate logical connection – 'St Francis got back and he had some followers as well'.

Once a sentence has been identified, a number of operations become possible. Its length in words can be calculated. It can be classified by function: statement, command, question, exclamation. Its formal properties can be noted and the sentence appropriately labelled: simple, compound, complex.

The next step down in unit size is to *clause*. For convenience and simplicity, this is to be understood in its traditional sense: a unit of language which contains one (and only one) finite verb or verb phrase. The distinction is made clear in two parallel sentences:

(1) On leaving the room, he slammed the door.
(2) As he left the room, he slammed the door.

Sentence (1) has only one finite verb (showing tense and mood) – 'slammed'. Sentence (2) has two – 'left' and 'slammed', and therefore is made up of two clauses.

Patterns in clauses may be explored by reference to the structures from which they are made. There are four of these elements: subject, predicator, complement (which includes direct and indirect objects), adjunct, abbreviated to S, P, C, A. Combinations of these elements offer the possibility of a great variety of clause patterns:

> They driver waved (SP)
> The boys waved back (SPA)
> One boy waved a handkerchief (SPC)
> Another gave the driver a cheer (SPCC)
> They threw their arms in the air (SPCA)

More common in the study of writing has been an examination of the status of clauses, classing them as independent or dependent. These terms refer to the ability of a clause to stand on its own or to need the support of another unit. In the sentence 'When the rain stopped, the sun quickly dried the pavements' only the second clause is free to operate on its own. 'When the rain stopped' is therefore a dependent or subordinate clause. These categories permit the description of sentences referred to earlier: a simple sentence consists of one independent clause, a compound sentence of two or more independent clauses, a complex sentence of one independent and at least one dependent clause.

In addition, each dependent clause may be distinguished by the function it performs. 'When the rain stopped', in the example above, is a clause acting as an adverb of time. Dependent clauses also serve as the equivalents of adjectives and nouns, with finer distinctions possible within each category.

Two further steps down in unit size (leapfrogging 'phrase' or 'group') brings us to *word*. The difference here from the study of words as vocabulary is that the function of each word is now the focus of attention. The labels are those made familiar in traditional grammar as 'the parts of speech': noun and pronoun, verb, adjective and adverb, preposition, conjunction.

At one time or another, all these methods of description (and many more) have been employed in the study of children's speech and writing. The difficulties inherent in defining some units have led to a variety of more or less ingenious substitutes for them. The slipperiness of 'sentence' has led some enquiries to avoid it altogether; others have devised new units to supplant it : T units (Kellogg Hunt), communication units (Loban). Another complication has been introduced in recent times with advances in the study of language. The terms used to describe patterns and structures in this section are, in the main, those associated with what has come to be called 'traditional' grammar. Markedly different approaches to the study of language are now being elaborated, notably the *transformational – generative* grammar associated with Noam Chomsky and the *systemic* grammar developed by Michael Halliday. Analysis of children's language on the basis of these models would differ in important respects from each other and from the traditional approach. (A limited experiment on a small sample of our children's writing was carried out, employing themes from systemic grammar. These are not reported here, but are discussed in some detail in the project's Final Report.)

Some readers may wonder whether any attempt has been made to establish a frequency count of grammatical constructions, to parallel that in vocabulary analysis. Once again, the indefatigable Thorndike (with three associates) provides an affirmative answer. 'An Inventory of English Constructions' offers frequencies of occurrence for 458 items, the result of analysing an extraordinary range of printed and written English. Unfortunately, its usefulness is limited by doubts on how representative this range of material is and by the unavoidable limitations on the number and kind of constructions considered.

In coming to select which features to study among the bewildering variety offered by the grammar of English, the enquirer is likely to be influenced by two major considerations :

(1) what evidence is there of its usefulness for my purpose?
(2) what hunches or intuitions do I have about features not previously investigated which might contribute something worthwhile?

Twelve items were finally chosen for application to the writing of the project children, by reference to these two rules, from an initial set of more than fifty. Of these twelve, six show firm evidence of their value as measures of progress towards mature levels of language skill. These are :

(1) average sentence length;
(2) average clause length;
(3) an index of subordination (subordinate clauses as a proportion of all clauses);

(4) a weighted index of subordination (the Loban index);
(5) the ratio of 'uncommon' subordinate clauses to all subordinate clauses ('uncommon' here means any clause which is *not* an adverbial clause of time nor a noun clause acting as object);
(6) a personal pronoun index – the number of personal pronouns per 100 words.

Two other features (the use of first and third person pronouns) raised interesting questions in relation to particular groups of children, and these will be considered, though in less detail than for the group of six, in Chapter 8.

The six tables which follow should be used with the precautions listed on pp. 53–4 very much in mind. Though not all the differences between figures in these tables are large enough to be significant in the statistical sense, they are all listed to exemplify the point made earlier that the rate of change is not even from year to year. Average figures for girls on all these measures are in advance of those for boys of comparable age, but the differences are relatively small by the end of the fourth year.

Table 2 *Average length of sentences in words*

Age group	C	CV	F	FV
1st year	8·7	8·4	9·4	9·0
2nd year	9·3	9·2	10·4	10·1
3rd year	9·8	9·7	11·0	10·5
4th year	10·1	9·9	11·4	10·7

Table 3 *Average length of clauses in words*

Age group	C	CV	F	FV
1st year	6·2	6·2	6·5	6·6
2nd year	6·3	6·5	6·9	7·0
3rd year	6·7	6·7	7·5	7·3
4th year	7·0	7·0	7·7	7·4

Table 4 *Index of subordination (as percentage)*

Age group	C	CV	F	FV
1st year	16·0	14·0	14·0	12·0
2nd year	19·0	18·0	16·0	16·0
3rd year	22·0	19·0	17·0	18·0
4th year	22·0	20·0	17·0	19·0

A brief explanation is necessary for the next measure. The subordination index of Table 4 is a relatively crude instrument for assessing complexity of structure, since it takes account only of the number of subordinate constructions and not of the way in which they are used. To make allowance for complexity of use, a modified system of scoring is required and Loban's weighted index is one of a number of possible solutions.

Thus a normal subordinate clause scores 1 point. If, however, it contains a verbal construction (by the use of a participle, infinitive or gerund) the score is 2. Two points are also scored if a subordinate clause is dependent on another subordinate clause rather than on the main clause. Extensions of this kind of construction lead to an appropriate increase in score value: a clause depending on a clause depending on a clause would score 3 and so on. Readers with the necessary perseverance might like to calculate the Loban index score for the final sentence of that children's favourite 'This is the house that Jack built.' A less protracted example is offered by the sentence 'If they arrive before I get back, ask them to wait.' The second subordinate clause depends on the first and scores 2. The sentence as a whole receives a score of 3, since the first clause counts 1.

One further operation is necessary. The longer a piece of writing the higher the score, so that division by number of words is vital. In the table below the resulting figure has been multiplied by 100 to give a score for every 100 words.

Table 5 *Loban weighted index of subordination score (per 100 words)*

Age group	C	CV	F	FV
1st year	2·9	2·6	1·8	1·9
2nd year	3·1	2·8	2·3	2·6
3rd year	3·7	3·3	2·5	2·8
4th year	3·8	3·4	2·8	3·0

Table 6 *Uncommon clauses as a proportion of all subordinate clauses (percentages)*

Age group	C	CV	F	FV
1st year	13	17	6	15
2nd year	21	18	18	24
3rd year	27	31	26	40
4th year	35	31	31	46

Table 7 *Personal pronoun index (number per 100 words)*

Age group	C	CV	F	FV
1st year	12·4	13·4	14·1	12·6
2nd year	11·8	12·9	11·8	11·4
3rd year	11·7	12·2	10·7	10·0
4th year	11·3	10·5	10·6	9·1

Analysis of writing and subsequent reference to these tables may be clarified by following the process through with an example piece. Michelle, whose cautionary tale on 'Fire' is reproduced, was 7·10 when the piece was written. It is classified as creative writing with minimum verbal stimulus. (The teacher struck a match and let it burn down to his fingers. When the class said it reminded them of fires, they were invited to write a story.)

Clause boundaries are shown by a single upright stroke; sentence boundaries by a double stroke. Finite verbs are in italics.

'Yesterday while me and all my family *were out* except my big brother/ our house *got* on fire//it *started*/when my big brother *was* in the kitchen//he *did not no*/that a piece of wood *had fell* onto the floor// it *set* the furniture on fire/and my brother *had to fetch* the fire brigade in a rush//then when my mum and dad and the family *came* home/they *wondered*/what *had happened*//then my brother *told* them/and now we always *put round* the guard.'//

There are 89 words in the piece, very close to the average registered in Table 1. With six sentences, the average sentence length is nearly 15, very much higher than the Table 2 figure. Clauses number 13, giving an average length of 6·8 words, beyond the third year level in Table 3. The five subordinate clauses among these produce a subordination index of 38, way beyond anything in Table 4. Curiously, since three are adverbial clauses of time and two noun clauses as object, there is no entry to Table 6. All five are first-order dependent clauses, scoring 1 point each. Converting the 5 points for the standard 100-word measure gives a figure for Table 5 of 5·6, again well beyond anything listed there. A total of 13 personal pronouns, adjusted to the 100 word standard, offers a pronoun index of 14·4, markedly higher than the average in Table 7.

The impression of a linguistically accomplished piece of writing is given substance by this examination. In addition, we are alerted to features that appear to contradict the maturity of Michelle's work.

Certain kinds of narrative writing seem to engender higher proportions of personal pronouns than is generally the case, so that this variation is less significant than it first appears. The absence of 'uncommon' subordinate clauses is a reminder that it is unwise to rely on a single piece of writing for evidence, because circumstances determine what kinds of subordination are necessary.

Nothing in this analysis is concerned with the quality of a piece of writing as a work of imagination and intelligence. What is described is there on the page as a defined set of structures and patterns. Using only the figures it is impossible to assert that a piece is good, bad or indifferent. The figures simply offer a guide to placing that writer's work on a series of scales of language maturity, a point made by the comments on Michelle's story. At the same time, the way language is used affects very powerfully our qualitative assessment. We are sharply aware of breadth and precision in vocabulary, of variety and complexity in sentence structure, of the degree of control over spelling and punctuation. In a subjective evaluation of writing these will attract very different emphases according to the preoccupation of the reader, the nature of the writing, the identity of the writer, but they will all carry some weight.

Sets of figures in tables are not exactly an eloquent testimony of the reality on which they are based. They are obviously artificial, referring to no one writer or piece of writing, but sketching an approximation to 'average' performance on a very limited number of dimensions. The truly 'average' piece of written work does not exist: even if every grammatical distinction were to be listed and measured, vocabulary and circumstances would be uncontrolled. The 'average' child or pupil is just such another convenient fiction.

Nevertheless, there is some profit in trying to demonstrate what such writing might be like, by using the scores as a guide and searching for those pieces which represent a reasonably close approximation to such an average.

This is, unsurprisingly, not a new idea. Professor Schonell in his book *Backwardness in the Basic Subjects* argued the case for establishing children's attainment levels in speech and writing. 'We should know what characteristics of their work are definite merits or weaknesses for their age, what common errors we can expect to eliminate by practice, and what faults will tend to right themselves simply through experience and maturation. We should know, too, what are the specific difficulties underlying different forms of composition – reproductive, narrative, imaginative and explanatory – and what are the characteristics of progress from age-group to age-group.' (Chapter 17, p. 364.) We might phrase this a little differently thirty-five years later, exercising perhaps a little caution over the use of the notion of error, but the central argument holds good, as do Schonell's recommendations to teachers: offer wide variety of experience, understand that writing is learnt by writing, provide constant encouragement, judge performance by age and not against some mechanical ideal standard.

He obtained, from a representative sample of 1,300 children aged from 7 to 14, four different compositions. The subjects of these were:

(1) story reproduction – 'Urashima, the fisher boy';
(2) narrative-descriptive – 'Home';
(3) imaginative – 'If you had wings and could fly, tell what you would do';
(4) explanatory – 'How to play . . . (any *one* game)'.

(Dennis Lawton followed this pattern, including the use of the same story text, in the investigation with secondary school children he reported in *Social Class, Language and Education*, 1968.)

For each age group, compositions were arranged in an order of merit by quality and a set in the middle of the order examined closely for content, structure and mechanical elements. Particular attention was paid to sentence structure – length, variety, use of co-ordination and subordination. On the basis of this examination, one piece was selected to serve as the median sample for that age group and kind of composition.

There is no possibility of an exact comparison with Schonell's results: for his children the topics for writing were highly specific; there was a thirty-minute time-limit for writing and he introduced qualitative features in making his selection. Nevertheless, for the language structures and 'mechanical elements', the performance of the 1970s children may be set alongside that of their predecessors of 1939, with these differences given due weight.

For the contemporary pupils, pieces of C or in one case CV writing were examined to discover those which came closest to matching the average figures on all twelve language measures (including the six listed in the tables earlier). No attempt was made to estimate whether they could be put forward as of 'average' quality in Schonell's sense.

In what follows, the Schonell median example for an age group, drawn from the 'imaginative' set of compositions, is placed first. Note that the writers of his compositions are three or four months younger than those representing the later group of children.

(Age 7½)
  'If I had wings and could fly. I would fly over the houses and fly over fensis. I would fly in the play in the playground and fly home to my mother and father and have my dinner and fly to scool.'

(Mark – aged 7.9, C writing)
  'once upon a time there was an old man called Mark Robbins and his frind culd David Wilson. David Wilson was very greedy about food. David was so greedy that he spent all of his money. Then they heard a small vuys say have three wishes. I towld David. He said I wish for 300 samgis and the coteg was filed with samgis. David started to eat them 1 by 1. I wish I was magick. I wish all the samgis are gone away. Siys of a mouse siys of a giyunt. Ho a mows Ha. My spel has worn out. Wake up David.'

(Age 8½)
  'If I had wings I would fly about in the sun-shine and play in the fields. I would fly over the tree tops high in the air. I could fly with the birds in the air every day.

  'I would play among the fiaries in the field too. If I where a fiary I would teach the rabits how to play games in the sun. I would play hide-in-seek round the trees in the wood. And I would be able to see all the little baby birds in there nest in the trees. I would fly and get my mothers erands every day.'

(Stephanie – aged 8.10, C writing)
  'one dark and stormy night I lay in bed unable to sleep I could hear the wind howlin and the house seemed to crec suddenly a blac shadow came past the window I scramed my dog came and my brother came a few minutes later the shadow was coming slow up my wall I screamed again but this time no body came to see what the matter was it came nearea and nearea and nearea and nearea up the wall it came so near that I put my head under the covers untill it was morning by that time the shadow had gone but there war the footstep there we was able to follow all the footseps.'

(Age 9½)
  'If I had wings I would fly over the sea and see all the fish's in the water. Then I could fly to school. I expected at first I would for-get they were on me, but I wonder how I would go to bed with them on. I have never seen anyone with any on but I would laugh if I did. But if I did have a pair, I would fly to Africa to see the black boys and girls. I would ask them if they would lend me some of their spears to show the boys in my class. Then I would fly over to Ceylon to get some of their

tea if they'v got any to spear. When I am over there the first thing I shall see is some bungalo's. Then I shall fly over to Scotland to see the kilts.'

(Darin – aged 9.9, CV writing)
'In Switsaland a year ago I went to Switsaland in one of the high villiages Nigel came with me it was a lovely day. We went to a villiage called Oberabrol it was high up in the masive mountains. One day me and Nigel were sking down a slop of a moutain. It was a cold day when Nigel tried acting up the slop of the moutain again. Then I came whoosh smack bang into Nigel. So we both tried geting up the slop of the moutain and avencherly we did it. We was so cold we went to the village again. It was quiet and a man came out of a house and said "come and have a hot drink with me" so we did. We had never heard or sen this man before we felt fritend when we got into his house and the man made hot drinks for us. Then the man saw a great cloud of snow dust the man yelled everybody started runing from the old man's hous the man fell and he got killed straight away. One of the reserch team men found the avalanche. Then they dug for people and 44 was killed.'

(Age 10½)
'If I had lovely gauzy wings I would soar right up into the sky and alight perhaps in quite a different place.

'It is a very cheap way of travelling because you don't have to pay. The first place I would go to would be a thick dence forest with trees knotted all over the place, the reason is because if any of my friends come with me we can have a game of hiding seek and hide in the hollow of a tree and we might even find a tresure box hidden in the branches.

'The next place I would go to would be Switserland where all the snowy mountains are, but I want to know how to get there. First I will go to the sea coast and follow a ship which says Going to Switserland. I fly after it and if I get tired I will board the ship when no one was looking. When I had recovered my breath I would start of again.'

(Raymond, aged 10.11, C writing)
'I am Special detective Charles Brown and I am investigating the mysterious journey at the under ground. Well it all started on the 11.30 train to Edinburgh the underground train set of at 11.30 and at 12 o'clock when it reached Edinburgh all the people had been gased. But there was a clue the ticket collector was missing So I got one man to identfea him. One man said he saw the man take a taxi to 30 Elm Road so I got the same man to take me there when I got there nobody was in

so I looked in a draw but at that moment CLUNK I was out. When I woke up I fond myself on a rubbish tip my face was all cut so I walked back to the basment and got the men to block all the foads and gave orders to look at people passports. The first one came along and one of the men saw the missing ticket collector so we caught him and took him to court he had a fair sentence because he was fond guilty of gasing the 11.30 passengers to Edinburgh.'

Some readers may like to undertake a structural analysis of both sets in order to see how nearly these children approach each other in the language resources they employ. Even without such close scrutiny, one point of comparison and one of contrast seem immediately striking:

(1) The rate of advance towards linguistic maturity speeds up noticeably from the second to the third year, a phenomenon already remarked on and exemplified in the tables.
(2) As Schonell makes clear in his commentary, many teachers in the 1930s expended great efforts on encouraging accuracy with the 'mechanical elements' – spelling, punctuation, paragraphing. In punctuation and use of paragraphs particularly, the two sets show clear differences, which may reflect a contrast in teaching priorities.

At this point, a return to the opening theme of the chapter is appropriate: how far are these children still language learners, as opposed to apprentices in writing? They are unarguably natives in the language; there is no evidence of 'un-English' English such as would be expected from learners with another language as their mother tongue. At the same time we would assert, for a variety of reasons, that the writers had not reached adult mastery of the written language. None of the evidence so far, however, has indicated the *absence* of structures or patterns; only continuing development in length, complexity and variety of some fundamental forms. In part, this is of course the result of the initial selection of grammatical items for study; if they are in some way the basic components of the language they will be present in a very high proportion of cases, if not in all.

It is perhaps in exploring the different ways in which meanings can be realised that children differ most from adults. They often seem to have one solution only, an all-purpose tool pressed into service on all occasions. The example has already been quoted of perhaps the most striking of these; 'and' as a universal co-ordinator, even when no co-ordination of that kind is needed.

In the speech of young children the arrangement of events and objects in long chains is striking. John, a 4-year-old, recalling an outing, will stand as representative for a universal practice:

'I went to the zoo and I went with daddy and I had a ice-cream and I saw a stripy horse and a man throwed fishes and we went to the tigers and we had some fizz in a paper cup and . . . and there was a old donkey and two baby goats and we came home on the bus.'

The usefulness of 'and' in joining equal units seems to be realised early in speech development. By the time children come to write it is a powerful habit, which gives way only slowly and reluctantly to the very large number of different joining methods provided for in English. Reference was made earlier in this chapter, in discussing the problem of identifying sentences in children's writing, to their ways of using 'and'. The three 'guiding principles' listed there are attempts to provide a solution to the difficulty of deciding when this conjunction is being used for one of its logical–sequential purposes and when it has none of this structural weight – a 'habitual' or 'textual' *and*.

Adults are aware of the variety of functions for which they employ this most useful of words, though they might be hard put to enumerate them all. Some common ones in joining clauses are:

(1) The sun shone and the breeze rustled the leaves (simultaneous events: an additive or cumulative process);
(2) The rains descended and the floods came (cause-effect: an illative or inferential process);
(3) She cleaned the shoes and put them on (chronological sequence).

In each case, the intended meaning may also be realised by subordinating one element to the other:

(1s) While the sun shone, the breeze rustled the leaves.
(2s) Because the rains descended, the floods came.
(3s) After she cleaned the shoes, she put them on.

While the second set of sentences are generally equivalent in meaning to the first set, most speakers or writers would feel, without necessarily pinpointing the structural difference, that they are not exact equivalents. The subtleties of these relationships, as of the whole English co-ordination–subordination system, are mastered only after long acquaintance with the language; some variations may elude all but those consciously concerned with the full range of stylistic effects attainable.

The argument is easily extended to each of the two other major co-ordinators:

(4)   She was poor but she was honest.
(4s) Though she was poor, she was honest.
(5)   Let me be the bowler, or I'll take my bat away.
(5s) If you don't let me be bowler, I'll take my bat away.
      or   If you let me be bowler, I'll not take my bat away.
      (where subordination and negation are necessary)

A detailed study of the steps by which children move from the relatively clumsy joining devices of their early language explorations towards the power and sophistication of the adult system would be extremely rewarding. Only an occasional glance could be spared for this in our investigation, but some oblique evidence is provided by examining the kinds of subordination these children resorted to in their writing and their frequency of use.

The reference earlier to 'uncommon' subordinate clauses as a measure of language maturity established the assumption that 'common' clauses existed, namely noun clauses as object and adverbial clauses of time. How common are they? Taking the case of adverbial clauses first, these turn out to represent a very consistent proportion of all the subordinate clauses employed: between forty-three and forty-six in every hundred right across the age range from 8 to 11. Equally consistent within this group is the degree of dominance established by clauses of time. For every two time clauses, the expectation would be that only one of all the other kinds of adverbial clauses would appear.

Because narrative, a sequence of events in time, is a very common form of writing in school, this should come as no surprise, though the consistency of its popularity may be. After clauses of time, the order of frequency of use runs – cause, condition, place, result, purpose (these last two are sometimes difficult to distinguish in children's writing), manner, degree, concession. This order matches that found in a number of earlier enquiries into children's writing, which suggests that different writing demands are in this case less important than the ready availability of these resources. When children look for ways of expressing their meanings accurately, some of these structural answers are much less accessible than others. The subordinate equivalents to 'and' and 'or' – time, cause, condition – head the list by frequency of use. Concession, the counterpart of 'but', is very rare: for 8-year-olds occurring once for every 130 time clauses, for the 11-year-olds, once for 60.

The conclusion is not that pupils find little use for the construction, but that the level of thinking for its full employment is reached comparatively late, probably in mid-adolescence. It is tempting, but dangerous in the absence of detailed evidence, to link its development as a language resource with the change, in Piaget's terms, from concrete operations to formal operations in levels of thinking. Unlike conditional clauses, where the circumstances joined together are dependent on each other:

'If you follow the instructions, you must win'

the concession clause sets up a contrast between circumstances; there is an element of surprise:

'Though he fished hard all day, he caught nothing.'

The relationship expressed by more complex forms such as

'Even if he pays me well, I will not take the job'

(which combines the properties of condition and concession) does not appear at all in this formulation in the writing. A number of approximate equivalents are possible:

'Pay me as much as you like. I will still not take the job.'

But these seem to be even less common than true concession clauses.

The preponderance of noun clauses as object over all other kinds is even more marked than the position of time clauses among adverbs. In narrative, verbs of saying, thinking, feeling (and many others) occur very frequently and often generate subordinate clauses. Two kinds are worth distinguishing: direct and indirect speech.

'He shouted to his mother, "I'm going out to play." '
'He shouted to his mother that he was going out to play.'

One regular phenomenon in children's writing is their early delight in reproducing dialogue directly, which gradually changes to indirect representation. One measure of this change is provided by the incidence of one kind of object clause by contrast with the other.

In the junior school first year, direct speech clauses outnumber indirect in the proportion $2\frac{1}{2} : 1$. By the second year the balance is moving towards equality of the two kinds and the changeover point occurs early in that year of accelerated changes, the third. By the fourth year indirect clauses are ahead of direct by 3 : 2. The numbers of other noun clauses (subject, complement, opposition, prepositional) are tiny by contrast. First-year writers produce 25 object clauses for one of all other kinds combined. By the fourth year, the ratio is down to 10 : 1. One variety, the subject clause, is a rarity throughout the junior school years, never appearing more than once for every 150 noun clauses. It is not exactly common in anything other than the most formal adult writing despite the popularity among advertisers of the formula 'What we want is . . .' As a method of providing distinctive emphasis for a statement it is one of many possibilities and far from the most obvious in a child's eyes. 'They want food' would be intensified as 'They do want food' much more readily than as 'What they want is food'.

The last of the subordinate clause kinds is the adjectival or relative clause. We were particularly concerned not only to discover how children dealt with the major choice offered, between restrictive and non-restrictive relative clauses, but also to chart the steady advance in adjectival clause use over the junior school years, reported in other enquiries. This change in the pattern of subordinate clause choice shows up clearly in the writing. As children move up the junior school they use subordination more and more freely, but in doing so they reduce the emphasis on noun clauses and compensate for this by employing adjectival clauses more often. Table 8 gives the details of this movement in emphasis.

Table 8 *Kinds of subordinate clause (as percentage of all subordinate clauses)*

Age group	Noun	Adjective	Adverb
1st year	46·0	11·0	43·0
2nd year	38·0	16·0	46·0
3rd year	36·0	19·0	45·0
4th year	34·0	22·0	44·0

One explanation of the early uncertainty with adjectival clauses was suggested by Lou La Brant (in 'A Study of Certain Language Developments in Children'). She examined examples occurring in the writing of nearly 500 children and concluded that difficulty in handling the relative pronouns was the most likely cause. When we consider some of the puzzles set by deciding between 'who' and 'whom', even for adults, her proposition seems eminently sensible, though it is probably only a partial explanation. Children may not feel a need for the structure until they have established other kinds of post-modification. 'The man in the grey suit' on this assumption would invariably precede 'The man who was wearing the grey suit'. A translation to the pre-modifying equivalent, 'The grey-suited man', might be guessed to occur later still, but that is a guess, since there is no detailed evidence to support it.

The difference between restrictive and non-restrictive uses is of some significance in language and meaning. The word modified by the clause may already have been identified, or alternatively it may need identification. In the first case the clause acts non-restrictively, in the second it is restrictive. Consider the two sentences:

(1) My brother who lives in Luton is an engineer.
(2) My brother, who lives in Luton, is an engineer.

In sentence (1) the clause 'who lives in Luton' identifies one particular brother (and not the others who may live in London or Brighton). In sentence (2), a similar clause is used to give additional information about a brother who is already identified (perhaps earlier in the writing) or who is unique; the *only* brother of the speaker. The non-restrictive clause is conventionally signalled in writing by being enclosed in a pair of commas. The message is 'this is useful, but not essential information'. In the second sentence the clause can be taken out and still leave the meaning clear. This cannot be done in the restrictive case.

Junior-school children, understandably enough, are not masters of this convention of punctuation, but close scrutiny of the writing context in which these clauses occur provides the evidence for classifying most of them with some confidence. First- and second-year children divide their attention equally between restrictive and non-restrictive clauses, but as adjectival clauses become more prominent in the third and fourth years, the non-restrictive becomes the favoured choice, outnumbering the restrictive by almost 2:1 at the age of transfer to secondary schooling.

No wholly satisfying explanation of this change of emphasis can be offered. One possibility is that with growing confidence in their writing skill, children begin to experiment with what they recognise as a useful, but essentially 'decorative', structure, employing other methods, perhaps pre-modification, to take the burden of 'restrictive' meaning. Many of these children certainly show a fascination for the accumulation of detail in description. Nine-year-old Janet's 'those old, tangled, mossy, twisted branches creaking in the wind' is a not-uncommon example of the pleasure in finding new ways to play the language game. They were still hidden from her eighteen months before. 'My little dog Kim is brown and he barks a lot and he has a fury coat and a red collar with his name on.' Perhaps the extra deliberations and emphasis of the relative clause makes it seem at first a very important feature, giving the non-restrictive form pride of place. With familiarity, and an ever-growing range of resources to select from, a child writer adjusts his valuation of this structure to permit greater flexibility of use.

One final detail is worth adding to this portrait of the developing child writer extending the range and assurance of his mastery in realising meanings through subordination. This is a general portrait, partaking of the characteristics of all the children whose work is under scrutiny. How much do individual children vary in each direction from this centre? In one sense, of course, the answer is 'enormously', as earlier reference to the uniqueness of individual development insisted. At the mature end are children who make use of most of the possibilities freely and accurately, producing writing different only in degree, not in kind, from that of adults. Their counterparts, the writing novices, provide evidence of the effect of age and maturity in gaining access to the subordination system.

Of the 290 children producing writing for the first year's collection, only six used no subordinations at all: five in the first-year group and just one second-year boy. In the final collection, when the children were completing their second, third and fourth junior-school years, all used subordination in at least one piece of writing. Three of the original six (including the solitary second-year child) employed it in only one piece. They were joined in this respect by three second-year children, each of whom had used subordination in only one of their first-year pieces.

For this small minority of children, entry to the subordination system is a hesitant process and the restriction this imposes on their writing is inescapable: they rarely, if ever, find other methods to produce an equivalent effect. All statements have equal weight, with relationships among them undeveloped. Karl, a $9\frac{1}{2}$-year-old, was one of a group asked to write about an aspect of a half-term project on 'Crops' as part of the concluding activities. He chose 'Soil'.

'Nitrogen runs thogh soll it is a gas is can not Bern or kill you it gives the ptants air ther are threelaors of soil clay lram and good soil Nitregen came from soll you cane not see it.'

The implications of this for the teacher concerned to aid children in their struggles with language will be taken up again in a later chapter.

INFLUENCES ON WRITING DEVELOPMENT

In an effort to explain why one child's writing differs from another's in its selection of language structures, attention has naturally enough been fixed on the effects of age. The idea of development in writing depends on the assumption that, with practice and growing maturity, advances in skill will take place. Equally obviously, this is not the whole story; reference has already been made to the fact that these advances do not occur at a steady rate over the junior-school years. If age and practice were the only influences, the written language level of any one 9-year-old would be much like that of any other. Children exposed to the same classroom environment would move forward more or less identically. Yet the reality is very different. Some children seem to advance very little over considerable periods of time (a phenomenon examined more closely in Chapter 8). Others appear to mark time for months and then accelerate with startling rapidity to overhaul their peers. What other influences are at work to explain these complex variations in performance?

(a) *Sex*
As the note earlier in this chapter indicated, girls write on average more than boys. It was suggested there that the difference was of the order of 10 per cent, but this again is an average figure. The differences are rather wider in the earlier years, but, by the stage of consolidation in year 4, they have become very much reduced. A similar result emerges when the pattern of structural choices is scrutinised.

In the history of enquiries into language acquisition during this century, the consistency of this advantage for girls is rarely challenged and then only in very limited sets of circumstances. Dorothea McCarthy, one of the most accomplished American investigators of this aspect of child development, provided a neat and authoritative summary in the chapter 'Language Development in Children' in the *Manual of Child Psychology* (edited by Carmichael): 'Whenever groups of boys and girls are well matched in intelligence and socio-economic background and when the situation in which language responses are recorded does not tend to favour the interests of one sex or the other, there appear slight differences in favour of girls.' After noting that girls start to talk earlier than boys, that they are quicker in making speech comprehensible and in general produce more language than boys she reaffirmed her point: 'there is convincing proof that a real sex difference in language development exists in favour of girls'.

That this is not quite the whole story appears in a symposium twelve

years later, in 1966 (published as *The Genesis of Language*, edited by
F. Smith and G. A. Miller). Mildred Templin, one of the contributors,
noted that 'many recent studies of the amount of verbal output and of
various grammatical characteristics show much less sex differentiation
than studies in the 1930s'. Whether this indicates a slowing-up by girls,
an acceleration by boys or a change in the design and conduct of enquiries is impossible to answer. The differences remain, if reduced, and
need to be taken into account in dealing with children's writing.

In Table 9, the magnitude of this advantage can be seen for the
children in our sample. For this illustration, the results for all age
groups and kinds of writing have been combined : the figures therefore
represent the situation for writing in general at the beginning of the
third junior school year. The variables listed as 1–6 are those treated
separately in Tables 2–7, i.e. sentence length, clause length, subordinate
index, Loban index, uncommon clauses, pronoun index.

Table 9 *Sex differences – mean figures on six language variables*

Variable	1	2	3	4	5	6
Girls	9·9	6·9	18·5	3·1	26·5	12·0
Boys	9·5	6·8	16·5	2·8	23·0	11·6

None of these differences is statistically significant, though for
sentence length and Loban index (variables 1,4) this is closely ap-
proached. Only in the use of personal pronouns is the difference in the
unexpected direction. By the end of the fourth year, the advantage for
girls is smaller still (though they have by then achieved equivalence in
the use of pronouns), with one notable exception. In their use of subordination (variables 3, 4) they maintain their lead.

If the differences are relatively small, they are consistent in direction,
a point worth remembering in setting our expectations for boys and
girls of similar ages and general abilities.

(b) *Measured Ability*
In order to arrive at objective assessment of intellectual capacity for
the children in our enquiry, two tests were employed. The first, Raven's
Progressive Matrices, is normally described as a 'non-verbal' test; that is
language plays no part in the test items themselves, which require, in
Raven's words, 'observation and clear thinking' for a successful solution. The second, the English Picture Vocabulary Test 2, is designed to
assess levels of listening vocabulary (and indirectly verbal ability).

Taken together, scores on these tests offer a reasonable estimate of general ability.

Children taking part in the enquiry completed these tests on two occasions: first at the beginning of the two-year period and again towards the end. Scores achieved were standardised to take account of age and the results were used to form six groups: high scorers on both tests, high scorers on the verbal test, high scorers on the non-verbal test, average performers on both, low scorers on both, all others. For the purposes of illustration here, the two extreme groups are the most enlightening.

Since verbal ability is one component of the tests, it would be surprising, even alarming, if differences failed to appear in the writing of these two groups. What matters is the size and nature of these variations. The high scoring (both tests) group produce much more writing than their counterparts with low scores: 3,700 words each over five collections against 2,000. Differences on the language measures are again best demonstrated in tabular form, with performance in each of the years listed to show both level of performance and rate of progress.

Table 10 *Differences between extreme test score groups*

Variable	1	2	3	4	5	6
High 1970	10·3	6·9	19·0	3·4	27·0	11·1
High 1971	10·4	7·2	21·0	3·6	36·0	10·1
Low 1970	8·7	6·6	12·0	2·2	15·0	12·2
Low 1971	8·9	6·7	14·0	2·5	19·0	12·0

At first sight these figures might be taken as an illustration of the resoundingly obvious: able children are much more advanced in their written language development than the less able. There are, though, three benefits to be obtained from the comparison:

(1) the magnitude of the advantage possessed by the able group is dramatically underlined; there is a difference in developmental stage of nearly three years;
(2) the consistency of advance by the able group and its moderate size over two years reinforces the earlier suggestion of a phase of consolidation in language development towards the end of the junior school years;
(3) the discussion of the effects of social class membership, in the next section, depends crucially on the implications of these results.

The usefulness of measures of ability like those described here lies in their predictive value. If we are given a set of test results, we are able to say with some confidence what level of writing performance might be expected, measured by the language features used. The reverse is also true. Given a piece of writing, analysed for the components we are concerned with, we should be able to estimate the likely test performances of the writer. The 'average' performances reproduced and discussed earlier in this chapter provide a convenient check. As 'average' performers, their writers ought to have average test results – and so they do, though Mark, the first-year representative, is at the upper limit of that average band and is beyond it if the verbal test only is considered.

(c) *Social Class Membership*

An awareness of differences in language use among people in different circumstances is manifest throughout the history of language study. Terms such as accent and dialect emphasise the effects of geography; register focuses on the use of language in particular situations. A concern with the influence of social, cultural and educational circumstances is also well documented. McCarthy, in the survey referred to earlier, traces this interest back well into the nineteenth century, where observations tended to be at best impressionistic, at worst absurd in their conclusions. Such were the efforts of those who 'established' the vocabulary of farm workers at a level attained by all normal children at three years of age.

In more recent times such work has been both more extensive and much better documented, though no less contentious for that. The origins of the great upsurge in interest, starting in the 1950s, are in part to be found in the proposition that language and educational failure are causally connected. Successive Government Reports (Early Leaving 1954, Crowther 1959, Robbins 1963) identified the wastage of talent in the educational system and pointed to social class for an explanation. What was needed was an hypothesis linking social class, language and education together in a coherent form, and one was forthcoming.

The importance of Basil Bernstein's theoretical and practical investigations in shaping educational policy and practice is undeniable. Their bulk and complexity, with the controversy they aroused and continue to generate, make any attempt at summary in a restricted space an impossible undertaking. Interested readers will find the collected papers in *Class, Codes and Control* (two volumes, 1971, 1973) an invaluable source, not least for Bernstein's wry and disarmingly honest assessment of his work in the Introduction to Volume 1. Critical commentaries, of varying levels of acidity, are represented in the writing of Lawton, Coulthard, Labov and Rosen, listed in the Bibliography at the end of this book.

The labels 'elaborated code' and 'restricted code' have now passed into educational folk-lore, more often misunderstood and misinterpreted than not. Though Bernstein has continued to modify details in the use of these terms, an explanation from a 1962 paper ('Social Class, Linguistic Codes and Grammatical Elements') establishes their fundamental form:

'The codes themselves are thought to be functions of different forms of social relations or more generally qualities of different social structures. A restricted code is generated by a form of social relationship based upon a range of closely-shared identifications self-consciously held by the members. An elaborated code is generated by a form of social relationship which does not necessarily presuppose such shared, self-consciously held identifications with the consequence that much less is taken for granted. The codes regulate the area of discretion available to a speaker and so differently constrain the verbal signalling of individual difference . . . The effect of this on speech for the restricted code is to simplify the structural alternatives used to organise meaning and restrict the range of lexicon choice . . . An elaborated code is part of the life chance of members of the middle class; a middle-class individual has access to the two codes, a lower-working-class individual access to one.'

Bernstein examined contrasted social-class groups for evidence of this difference in speech; Dennis Lawton extended the enquiry to writing. In these early studies the subjects were adolescent boys (though later work extended the range considerably). In both cases, social class differences in language use emerged, independent of ability, and the differences were observed to increase with age.

All the children in our experiment were placed, by reference to fathers' occupation, in one of the five categories of the Registrar-General's system of classification. The proportion of the whole sample in each category corresponded very closely with the national figures, providing further evidence of the representativeness of our children. To test the language difference theory, those children in Classes I and II (whose fathers were in professional, managerial, executive occupations) were contrasted with those in Classes IV and V (fathers in semi-skilled or unskilled occupations).

If the effects of access to a restricted code only are, in Bernstein's words, 'to simplify the structural alternatives used to organise meaning', the performance of these two groups, on our language measures, should be markedly at variance, with the IV and V group producing the more 'immature' results.

Table 11 *Differences between contrasted social class groups*

Variable	1	2	3	4	5	6
I, II 1970	10·2	6·7	19·0	3·2	26·0	11·6
I, II 1971	10·4	7·2	22·0	3·4	38·0	10·7
IV, V 1970	9·2	6·9	13·0	2·3	17·0	12·2
IV, V 1971	9·5	6·8	17·0	2·9	22·0	12·5

The differences are considerable, as the table indicates, but not as great as those between the two extreme test score groups (Table 10). They are, too, in the expected direction. Proof of the hypothesis on the effects of social class on language development? Clearly not, when the influence of measured ability is taken into account. The test results of the IV and V group enable a comparison to be made with the language performance of groups formed on the basis of their test scores. When this is done, the lower-social-class group of children is seen to perform *much as their test scores suggest they ought to.* The correspondence is not exact, hinting that social class membership might produce some minor effects. The most obvious example in the table is the result for variable 6 (personal pronoun index), where the use of personal pronouns by the IV, V group goes against the general trend in becoming slightly more frequent, not less, in the course of time.

An irrefutable explanation of this result, which goes counter to much of the published evidence, is impossible. The age of the children may be significant, remembering Lawton's conclusions, with his 12- and 15-year-old boys, that the effects of social class increased with age. Yet P. R. Hawkins's investigation into the speech of 5-year-old children concludes 'we have shown very considerable differences between the type of speech produced by middle-class children and that of working-class children, which may well have important cognitive consequences'. Of significance here, in view of the comment made above on personal pronoun use, is the finding that 'working-class children . . . tend to use pronouns instead of nouns as "heads" ', that is as the key word in a nominal group – for example 'boy' in 'that tall, nine-year-old boy'.

A more persuasive case may be made out for the situation in which the language is produced. William Labov demonstrated this forcefully (in his monograph 'The Logic of Non-Standard English') in describing two interviews with Clarence, an 8-year-old Harlem child. By making the situation less threatening, less formal, the interviewer was able to get very much closer to a true view of the boy's capacity for language. Children who are the subjects of research are frequently placed in unaccustomed surroundings, confronted by strangers, set novel tasks for purposes which often remain obscure. Our writers were in their own school, with a familiar teacher, tackling writing tasks which were closely related to those they knew well from past experience.

As usual, there is evidence which casts doubt on this more plausible suggestion. Elizabeth Hitchfield, in *In Search of Promise*, concerned herself specifically with a group of high-ability children drawn from the National Child Development Study. Her fellow worker, Mrs James, analysed the speech children produced during interviews, using parts of the analysis systems of Lawton and Loban. Her conclusion was that, for this able group of children, measured ability was a better predictor of grammatical usage than social class. Perhaps for these children, who have been studied from birth onwards, the interview situation was less strange because of their awareness of their special position.

No easy solution is possible in trying to resolve this complex issue. Children are affected, in the way they use language, by the social and cultural environment in which their language has developed, but to a smaller extent than might be expected. Differences are detectable in their writing, but they are too scattered and too specific to permit any confidence in the conclusion that two distinguishable *styles* or *codes* in language exist to explain them. We may be approaching the question with the wrong emphasis, using inappropriate analytic tools, as Professor Halliday argues in his Foreword to *Class, Codes and Control*, Volume 2:

'Language is central to Bernstein's theory; but in order to understand the place that it occupies, it is necessary to think of language as meaning rather than of language as structure . . . Every normal child has a fully functional linguistic system; the difficulty is that of reconciling one functional orientation with another. The remedy will not lie in the administration of concentrated linguistic structure. It *may* lie, in part, in the broadening of the functional perspective – that of the school, as much as that of the individual pupil. This in turn demands a broadening of our own conceptions, especially our conceptions of meaning and of language.'

(d) *Patterns of Behaviour*
One necessary ingredient in assembling a full profile of each child undertaking writing for us was some description of that child's charac-

teristic ways of behaving in school. Dr D. H. Stott's 'Bristol Social Adjustment Guide' was finally selected as a convenient method of detecting malajustedment or unsettledness in school. For the teachers completing it there was the advantage of speed and ease of application, with no additional expert knowledge needed beyond their professional skill and experience. Scoring, for our purposes, was also uncomplicated. The Guide produces a tally of adverse items and their number determines the category best describing the child : 0–9 – stable; 10–19 – unsettled; 20+ – maladjusted. The total score is capable of being further analysed into fifteen sub-categories, each defining a particular kind of behaviour or attitude, but this refinement was not employed because the attention was on groups rather than on individuals in the first stage of the investigation.

The effect of instability on writing performance is again best demonstrated by contrasting what the two extreme groups achieve. The 'stable' group produced 3,200 words each on average over the five collections; the 'maladjusted' group 2,100. The figure for the extreme ability groups, quoted earlier, was 3,700 : 2,000; for the contrasted social class groups, 3,600 : 2,400.

Table 12 *Differences between extreme social adjustment groups*

Variable	1	2	3	4	5	6
Stable 1970	10·0	6·9	17·0	3·0	23·0	11·6
Stable 1971	10·2	7·0	20·0	3·4	33·0	11·5
Maladjusted 1970	8·7	6·5	12·0	2·2	15·0	12·5
Maladjusted 1971	9·0	6·7	15·0	2·5	24·0	11·6

In comparing Table 12 with Tables 10 and 11, the size of the contrasted groups must be taken into account. The test score and social-class groups are relatively small and roughly equal in size; the 'stable' group covers almost two-thirds of all the children, the 'maladjusted' barely one-fifth. Nevertheless, most of the differences are large and all are in the expected direction. Some encouragement can be found, though, in the rate of development achieved by the disturbed children over the two years – see especially variables 5 and 6 in relation to the lowest test score group's performance (in Table 10).

Once more the interpretation of such results is made difficult by the way that these measures of children's capacities, behaviour and circumstances are intertwined. Poor performance on the tests is linked strongly with patterns of behaviour and this in turn with social-class membership. But how are causes and effects to be distinguished and the directions determined? A child may behave in school in ways that suggest a degree of maladjustment, but school itself may be a cause. Inability to meet school expectations of performance and progress could trigger abnormal behaviour: withdrawal, depression, anxiety, hostility, reslessness, a total lack of confidence. Equally we may look to the home as causative agent: a clash of cultures where attitudes and patterns of behaviour in some sense rewarded at home are inimical to school success.

A fully satisfying solution to this question is probably out of reach in the present state of our knowledge. An explanation is almost certainly to be found in the complex processes of interaction among all these influences, though the effects of ability are likely to be a dominant feature. For teachers, concerned to provide the most effective help for their pupils, one valuable pointer to action emerges. Behaviour difficulties tend to decrease with age without any direct intervention, a fact which helps to explain the progress of the maladjusted group shown in Table 12. Attention to the less intractable of these problems, with accompanying adjustments to organisation and method in the classroom, could conceivably accelerate this change – given, of course, classes of moderate size and appropriate physical conditions and resources. This point is taken up in greater detail in Chapter 8, when other evidence on characteristic behaviour patterns is examined.

(e) *Size of Family, Position in Family*
In what has now become a classic study of children's educational progress, J. W. B. Douglas followed the fortunes of more than 5,000 children from birth through the years of formal schooling, with the primary aim of establishing the dimensions of what came to be called 'educational wastage' against the background of those children's homes and schools. The report on their first twelve years of life, published as *The Home and the School* in 1964, has two chapters devoted to the effects of completed family size and position in family on children's educational achievements. On family position, Douglas concluded that only children showed few, if any, advantages over the eldest child in families of two or three. The eldest child tended to improve his test scores between the ages of 8 and 11 in relation to his younger brothers and sisters and did better than expected in selection examinations at 11, while the later born did worse. For family size, the conclusion was related to social class membership. To quote Douglas: 'In the middle classes, it is only the child from a large family of four or more who is handicapped, whereas in the manual working classes the children are progressively handicapped with every increase in family size.'

The writing performance of our group of children tends to confirm the first finding. Eldest and only children are very much alike in output and in scores on the language variables. More interesting is the fact that they are very little different from children in other family positions : youngest or intermediate. On the few occasions where sizeable differences emerge, these are more convincingly explained by reference to ability than to birth order.

With family size, the effect of measured ability again complicates interpretation. Children from small families (one or two children) seem to do better than those from large ones (five or more children), but the differences are far from universal and are better attributed to ability and behaviour patterns than to family size. Indeed, the children from large families perform in some ways rather better than their test scores suggest they might, which offers an unexpected gloss on Douglas's conclusion.

(f) *Handedness*

The opportunity was taken of comparing the efforts of left-handed writers with their right-handed counterparts, not least because many teachers have a wide variety of views on these 'awkward' children. There were 33 in the group of 290 children, 22 boys and 11 girls. While the sex ratio matches figures from a number of investigations, the total number is considerably higher than is to be expected : about 7 in every 100. The difference is brought about by the inclusion of so-called 'mixed'-handers in the group. A 'pure' left-hander is defined by reference to the favoured hand in a range of carefully differentiated tasks, of which writing is only one.

Left-handers have been found to perform better on average than right-handers in verbal tests and ours were no exception. They also outperformed right-handers on the non-verbal Matrices. With ability a powerful determinant of writing development, they should have demonstrated a clear advantage, but this failed to appear. Their output was identical with that of right-handed children and their scores on the language measures were higher on only three variables (1, 2, 6) and then not by as much as their test scores would have suggested.

There is no real difficulty in finding an explanation for a decrease in fluency. A left-handed child in a conventionally right-handed world is at some disadvantages. In writing, the left to right direction is an inescapable obstacle. Why the fact of being left-handed should affect the language structures selected for writing is much less obvious. It may be that, with relatively young children, the physical difficulty of writing takes an abnormal share of the writer's attention, thus restricting the freedom to experiment syntactically. This is, though, no more than a very tentative speculation.

Though their teachers were aware of these left-handed pupils, none made any special provision for them – understandably enough, since all were performing at least adequately, set against the standards of their classmates. These results may suggest that some direct help would be beneficial: advice on writing stance and the position of paper, ensuring that these children have space to their left.

(g) *School and Teacher*
One of the teachers contributing the work of her pupils to the enquiry said, at the end of the last collection: 'Will we get a productivity bonus from Burnham if we show up as efficient teachers?' Relief at finishing a long and taxing job perhaps prompted this parting shot, but it may seem a not unreasonable question. With each child's progress in written language use carefully charted, a line back to the effectiveness of teaching organisation and method would appear a simple matter. However, if the preceding arguments on the tangled network of influences were not enough, the circumstances of the experiment prevent any unassailable answer. Children were taught by different teachers in each of the two years; sometimes as many as six, excluding supply teachers and students in training.

A less complicated but equally fruitless pursuit is to compare not teachers, but schools. Using each of the major language variables in turn, groups of schools appeared which seemed to promote development more than the remainder. They were, unfortunately, largely different schools each time and no common factor emerged to account for the results. Schools in each of these groups were both large and small, urban and rural, socio-economically favoured and not, old and new, with more or fewer than average able children.

A more detailed examination of changes over one year is beginning to hint at some of the qualities that may make for success. Among the more stable of these are:

(1) the degree of importance given to writing by a teacher, manifested in a number of ways – frequency, variety, treatment, progression;
(2) strong encouragement of 'free choice' reading as a major activity when other work is completed.

CONCLUSION

The evidence and accompanying arguments paraded in this chapter effectively prevent any neat conclusion. Age, ability and behavioural stability make important contributions to those developments in writing that have been selected for examination. Other influences are at work, though their effects are slighter and masked by the degree of inter-relationship among them. The most direct conclusion seems to be to let the children speak for themselves.

In the sequences which follow two ends are served. The first is to exemplify the changes that take place in a child's response to writing over time: the two collections are separated by sixteen months. The second is to provide as graphic an illustration as possible of the cumulative effects of the influences that so far have been discussed individually. On this last point a repetition of an earlier caution is necessary: no judgement of quality is implied in choosing these pieces. The writers stand for the oppositions of influences: older/younger, high/low measured ability, girl/boy, stable/unstable in school behaviour, favoured/less favoured social circumstances.

Ruth 9 years 9 months at the time of the first collection; 11.1 by the second. In top 2 per cent for scores on verbal and non-verbal tests. Very low social adjustment scores. Register-General's Class II.

1st collection
C Writing (From a picture of May Day celebrations in a country village.)

'One day when my friends and I where on the village green and a man brought out a maypole. We each took a ribbon and began to do the bankers pole then we plaited it and everybody who was there gave us a clap because not a speck of pole was showing. Then all of a sudden the maypole fell down a big hole and the people who were holding the ribbons went down as well. There was a saying about this village. It was that a long time ago a witch had once lived there and when she was about to die some elves came and asked if they could have the village when she was dead, she did not want to give it to them but it was in the rules. just before the witch died she put a spell on the village that one day the maypole would fall through a opening in the grass and that the village would fall a sleep for ten years. The time had come and the maypole had gone. After we had gone thourgh the opening in the grass we kept on falling for an hour. After that time we landed in a cave it was dark and wet. They let go of the maypole ribbons and held hands we tried to find our way out but did not succeed. Then I heard a sound it sounded like water running. We went towards it and we saw a stream. We followed it for about a mile and around the corner and we saw a speck of white it seemed to be a exit. We walked towards it and went out and looked around we saw a castle we went in and found a witch sitting on a chair. I put a spell on the village you live in it has occurred and in two years the other spell I put on your village will occur unless you do what I say. We said yes and she said you must move to a different place and let me have the village. We did not like it but she sent us back to tell the news we decided to kill her. We got back to the castle and asked a friendly giant if he could find the magic word which would break the spell and kill the witch somehow he found it the witch died and we went back and lived peacefully.'

CV Writing (From a discussion of words: 'hole', 'creature', 'odd' – children encouraged to write a story using one word as a focus.)

'There once was a man he lived in a house on some alotments. One day he was digging a hole for a tree. When he went home for tea he had not yet finished digging the hole. That evening after tea some boys came to play in the alotments when they found the hole. They went down into it and sat at the bottom and looked around – they did not see anything they looked again and a little door appeared they went up to it and pushed it opened. They decided to venture down into it. There were a small pair of ladders they climbed down and down. It seemed it would not end. They kept climbing and adventurly they saw a speck of light in the distance it seemed to be glowing yellow. They climbed on at great speed and adventurely reached the bottom When they were on the ground they looked around and saw a great book-shelf with huge books on it they took one of them down and had a look inside it seemed to be a magic spell book. They looked for a spell to take them back to England. Just then a witch came in and saw them looking in her book she said in a small squeakey voice what do you think you are doing with my spell book. The children told their story. After that the witch said you shall not get back to your world until you have been my slaves for a month. The children asked what to do first and the witch said if you go through that door you will come into giant land there you will met a giant with four arms who will try to catch you. Let him and you will at night chop off his head and bring it to me. They were given a sword and dish. They went through the door and met the giant. That night when the giant had gone to sleep they managed to cutt off his head. They put in on the dish and climbed up the trap and got back into the witche's house She got her spell book and found the spell and all four were back in England they climbed out of the hole and ran home and never went near that area to play again.'

F Writing (From individual topic work – summary for rest of class.)

'FOOD. Our farmers can produce enough food for only half of the people. Our farms produce nearly all our eggs, potatoes, milk and

vegetables that we need, but only half of the bacon, cheese, meat, butter
and other fats. Some goods we like such as bananas, tea rice and coffee
grow only in hot countries so they have to be imported.
'RAW MARETRIALS. Cotton and rubber cannot be grown in Britain so
they must be imported. Other countries send us all our petroleum and
nearly all our tin, copper, bauxite. We export sugar beet, wheat, meat,
eggs, butter, timber, wool, iron ore. We import sugar cane, cotton,
wheat, butter, meat, timber, iron ore, wool. The wheat we buy from
Canada is hard, for making bread. It will not grow here.'
FV Writing (Part of a series summarising the story of Easter, after discussion.)

'All the Disciples except two knew that Jesus was alive the Disciples
were in the upper room. The other two Disciples were on the road to
Emmaus from Jerusalem it was dark and the Disciples were miserable
then a stranger met them and the stranger asked the Disciples if it was
the road to Emmaus and if he could walk with them they answered yes
to both questions so the stranger walked with them When they got to
Emmaus they went to a room they had booked and the stranger broke
the bread all of a sudden the Disciples realised that it was Jesus. Then
they hurried to Jerusalem to tell the other Disciples the knews but they
did not know that the others already knew. When they got there they
told what had happened and the Disciples knew Jesus was alive. Then
in came Thomas he did not belive Jesus was alive and said not untill
I can touch his wounds will I belive. In a few days in that upper room
Jesus met Thomas and Thomas belive and fell on his knees.'

2nd collection
C Writing (From a request to describe loneliness, preferably in form of
a poem.)

'As lonely I sit by the fire,
I wonder if anyone will come?
My cat is my only friend, though he's not human.
I live too far away to be cared for
Confined to bed am I.

Every morning my son gets food and wood
But yet I do not see him he passes by
I sit out of bed each day not a word do I speak
except to puss
Only a little way can I walk

My thoughts are deep and wandering over long years past
for I am too old to find my young self again.'

CV Writing (Description of an imaginary ride, following a discussion on varieties of movement.)

'I had a pet giraffe his name wasn't decided but he understood me perfectly. When I first got him I went for a ride on his back for a day. I had some food with me. We started at eight o'clock. I told him to get down on the ground so I could climb up. He put his front legs wide apart and lowered himself. I climbed up and fell off I tried again and succeeded in getting on. I told him to move and he started to walk. The movement was a slow wobble from side to side and a little bit up and down he stopped and ate off a tree. We carried on and stopped again at a water hole he did the splits with his front legs and drank and at that moment he saw a lion. He got up cautiously and ran off I bounced up and down on his back and held on tight to his mane. He headed straight back home and hid in a shed I fell off and that ended our day.'

F Writing (From instruction : 'Choose a job you know well because you have watched someone doing it. Describe it, mentioning its good and bad points.')

'My dad is an english teacher he teaches only english. Nearly every week he brings home exam papers and seems to have no time to mark them but somehow he manages to keep up. The disadvantages are : he never has time to finish his building and if we say anything wrongly in speaking or spelling we get told off throughly. The advantages are getting days off through the union when he can build but it also means he dosen't get paid for that day. For a teacher you don't get much money and it is very hard to keep up.'

FV Writing (After a visit to the Lincolnshire Life Museum.)

'It was raining as we set off to the old Barracks were the Museum is now. We arived at 10.05 a.m. and took our coats off and went inside. The first room was just an introduction to the museum it had machines, jugs, pictures of old people and medals which workers from Rustons had won. We went up stairs to a room full of sports gear, things used for making butter and cheese and also some farming equipment. The next room had laundry implements and a post office which sold things like soap, sweets, tabacco and a few herbs to flavour food with there were also toys. We went down stairs again to a basket exhibition. Here are a few of the baskets we saw – washing, dilivery, farming, ice, potato, cod liver, picnic and bobin. We went outside into the rain and went into a transport shed it had about 16 coaches there an a 1882 hearse, plank sided wagon, sheriff's coach, brougham and carriers cart. Outside again we looked at the oldest letter box in Lincolnshire it came originally from Gosberton Bank. After that we trudged home in the rain and got absoletly soaked.'

David 7·10 at the time of the first collection; 9·2 by the second. In bottom 2 per cent for scores on both tests. High (in maladjusted range) social adjustment score. Registrar-General's Class V.

1st collection
C Writing (Asked to write down the things he liked to see.)
'I like to see a bat, a cat, a snowman, a lory, sowe flowers.'
CV Writing (Original stimulus two coloured pictures; one of children setting out on holiday, the other of children playing on a beach. David asked to write his own story, avoiding the pictures.)
'One day, Mel and me toce the dog for a woc and the dog ran a way and David an haft it and cot it and wet ham and had are tey.'
F Writing (From ITV programme 'Finding Out' on brown bears.)
'I wos to cubs and a mother bear. They bron bers.'
FV Writing (Pictures of elephants, discussed at length with the teacher.)
'I saw a elephent at it was drinkeing warter. Some people rid on the elephens back The elephent is bigg and has a long trunk it has tow big toks it is fat and it has fat legs.'

2nd collection
C Writing (From a coloured picture of Second World War planes in flight.)
'I am David an air man I drive a Lancaster one day the sirons wer going all the pilets climbed in to the aeroplan we toock of at 8 we went up and I drivd the pans we dropt boms on the hover plans aer hover aeropland was wit me three of are aeropland was bond a aeroplan got aer plan befor it hit aer I jumped hiwt how the areoplan on a parashot.'
CV Writing (Story following a visit to the local fire station.)
'One day I was trapt in a fire and the Fire men jumped in the Fire engin and went to the Fire and a Fire man shopped the door down and I ran out All fir was on me so I roled up in stand and it stopped. the bell went and the Fir men slid down the pole and jump in the Fire engine.'
F Writing (A description of the morning before going to school.)
'Some morning I wake up by an ilarm clock it was 8 o clock I got hawed of bed and ran down stairs my mum had my favouirite breakfest on the tabal it was weetabix I eated it and got washed and I got dressed and went to school.'
FV Writing (After the fire station visit and an extensive class discussion.)
'Yesterday are class went to the Fire station. We saw a ladder going up to a window and the Fire man climbed the lader and lowered the

dummy down on a ladder and we went into the Fire eighen and we saw some masks and the Fire men put them on we thay go into a Fire and the Fire man teld us that ther were 400 galons of water in the Fire eighin.'

5

Contexts for Writing

'I sought a theme and sought for it in vain,
I sought it daily for six weeks or so.'
(W. B. Yeats — *'The Circus Animals' Desertion*)

'I can't think of anything to write about.'
(Any pupil to any teacher)

One difference between Yeats and that imaginary but very real pupil is the difference in their understanding of, and response to, the situation of being faced with a blank sheet of paper and an injunction (from within or from some external source) to write. Yeats discovers, in the very act of being unable to write, material for a memorable poem. The struggle drives him to explore the springs of his own inspiration until, out of the process of exploring in and through writing, a solution appears.

'Maybe at last, being but a broken man,
I must be satisfied with my heart, although
Winter and summer till old age began
My circus animals were all on show,
Those stilted boys, that burnished chariot,
Lion and woman and the Lord knows what.'

He uses writing to survey the sweep of his experience as a writer and from it derives his answer; the vainly-sought theme is himself and he reluctantly, rather grimly, admits it in the final lines:

'I must lie down where all the ladders start,
In the foul rag-and-bone shop of the heart.'

A child, without Yeats's sixty years' experience of what writing can achieve, is too often left in the dark about what the business is for. The purposes of writing and the audience it is intended for remain unexplained or, in schools, interpreted very narrowly. During an investigation of the written language of secondary school pupils, a Schools Council Project team led by James Britton examined the nature of the audience for whom school writing was intended. A set of six categories was devised to apply to the written work collected. These were: (*a*) child to self; (*b*) child to trusted adult; (*c*) pupil to teacher as partner in dialogue; (*d*) pupil to teacher in a particular (educational) relationship; (*e*) pupil to teacher seen as examiner or assessor; (*f*) writer to his readers or public. In the fifth category fell not only writing in examinations, but all that produced to satisfy the teacher (frequently as a check on the efficacy of his teaching) and which the pupil expected to be used to assess the quality of his writing or the extent of his information. Even as early as the first year in the secondary school, writing for this audience accounted for 40 per cent of the whole, advancing to 61 per cent by year seven (these figures are taken from *Keeping Options Open*, one of a series of pamphlets produced by the Writing Across the Curriculum 11–13 Years Project, in which purpose and sense of audience are most informatively discussed).

The junior school pupil, protected to some degree from the influence of external examinations, may be less circumscribed in choice of audience, but the evidence of our own enquiry suggests that as much as one-third of his writing may have this narrow focus. Instead of writing being used as a vital part of the process of learning, in this form it becomes a technique for producing evidence of what has been learnt. What proportion is inescapably necessary for the teacher to monitor his own effectiveness is debatable, but these figures seem cripplingly high. If writing is to serve all its many important purposes, it must have freedom to do so.

To reassert a theme from an earlier chapter, speaking and writing are vital components in a child's intellectual, emotional and social development. In their transactional function they inform, advise, persuade, rework experience into new forms; when used expressively they allow the individual to relate himself to all he experiences. The process changes the speaker or writer; he is more conscious, more aware than he was before. Writing constitutes the act of perceiving the shape of experience *and* of reshaping it. So powerful an influence in education would be wasted if constrained to do less than it is capable of achieving.

Nothing in this argument is intended to reduce the importance of having something to write about. A theory of function and audience, no matter how elegant, is incomplete without reference to the experience which is to be worked on and aimed at a reader. Many teachers, and certainly the majority of those who collaborated with us in producing the writing, see choice of subject or starting point as the most formidable challenge, dominating all other concerns. 'What shall I get them to write about?' is the teacher's counterpart to the child's appeal with which this chapter opened.

Our group of teachers, faced with producing more than twenty situations for writing in six terms and restricted to some extent by the rules of the game, heaved a sigh of relief in unison at the end of the sequence. For some, to the admiration of the 'outsiders' waiting for the writing to appear, the challenge provoked a demonstration of a thoroughly professional skill. These teachers seemed never at a loss for ideas and allied their inventiveness to a concern that this 'special' writing should be an integral part of their classes' total programme of work. The impression to be gained from all these sequences of situations for writing is the extent to which each teacher can be said to possess an individual style of approach. There is an expected variation on a dimension that might be labelled 'adventurous-cautious', where the majority rely on success from past experience and a few explore un-tried possibilities. Some teachers are strongly verbal, others more likely to turn to sight or sound or activity in developing a setting for their pupils. Another difference is the degree to which each teacher makes explicit her expectations for the writing; a variation in the formality of the occasion.

Paradoxically, the very richness and variety of these occasions for writing conceal a real danger for the teacher. The eye and mind are taken by this diversity and fail to notice a restriction in the *kinds* of writing explored by pupils. This becomes most noticeable when 'crea-tive' writing is aimed at. To read the great range of writing collected for our enquiry is to be confronted by the realisation that children often see a single demand behind the variety of surface inducements to write. The writing stimulus, whatever its nature, becomes a springboard, lost sight of after its initial purpose is served. The most frequent outcome is, in functional terms, a loose kind of expressive writing, occasionally with narrative form, having 'I' as the centre. Expressive writing may be the source of all the differentiated mature functions, but opportuni-ties must be provided for the development to take place. On this analysis, some interpretations of 'creative' writing fail in this crucial purpose, while giving the appearance of success.

If an impetus is to be given to other kinds of writing, the obstacles need to be clearly recognised. The first of these is represented by the teacher's reluctance to interfere, to interpose some barrier between the experience and the writing that grows from it. As a response to the preset rigidity of old-style composition this was long overdue, but it seems to have become as inflexible an orthodoxy as the system it replaced, though not for all teachers.

The second difficulty is located in the nature of the stimulus offered and is best described as an opposition between open and closed, or convergent and divergent situations. Some examples will help to establish this argument. First, the power of association. Shortly after the film *2001* had been shown on television, a group of teachers experimented with fragments of its theme music (Richard Strauss's *Also sprach Zarathustra*) as a stimulus for writing in their junior school classes. Of 110 pieces, only 12 were not space fiction narratives. Teachers will undoubtedly have examples from their own experience of the more generalised effects of powerfully programmatic music – giants and magic emerging from *In the Hall of the Mountain King*, battles in variety from Beethoven's overture to *Egmont*, heroic adventures from Sibelius's *Karelia*.

Similar effects emerge when children are confronted with non-representational art; some configurations of shape, space, colour lead to a remarkable consensus of interpretation, others emphatically do not. In an earlier experiment, I asked an artist to produce six 'pictures', using black poster paint on white paper 22 inches by 15 inches, allowing himself not more than a dozen brush strokes for each. Groups of third-year juniors, third-year secondary pupils and students in higher education were then asked to talk about them or to respond to them in writing. One produced from all three groups near unanimity : it was 'about' the sea. One separated the youngest group from the others: they saw a haunted house; their elders variations on the themes of prison and loneliness. Two produced confused, sometimes hostile, reactions, usually ascribed to their apparent 'meaninglessness'.

The extent and nature of the teacher's involvement, linked with choice of stimulus, inevitably determine the way children set about the task of writing. Two project teachers, in different schools and working independently, chose to use the same picture, of fire-fighting in Jacobean times, as a starting-point for writing. Each had a brief class discussion to begin. One teacher then asked his group to 'write a story' about the picture and received in return a set of historical fictions, all but one in the third person. The other teacher extended the discussion to a consideration of the different ways in which the picture might be responded to. From this emerged not only the 'historical fiction' answer but also the 'eye-witness' or 'participant' method, involving a change of stance from third- to first-person narrative. A third suggestion was to itemise the content of the picture; a fourth to treat it in broadly aesthetic terms ('all the faces look alike and the colours are very dull'). One final possibility was to deal with the picture's historical significance ('in those days they didn't have proper fire-engines, or firemen either' – this from a boy who had come across an article on eighteenth-century fire insurance signs).

Clearly there can be no fixed rules to govern choice of stimulus or the ways in which a teacher creates an opportunity for writing. There are occasions when the teacher's job is to do no more than get out of the way; some kinds of personal writing demand this freedom if they are to survive at all. At other times, as in the last example, children need encouragement to explore the variety of legitimate ways of responding to experience. Finally there are instances when the teacher needs to be directive, to make sure a particular purpose is served by the writing – in selecting and ordering observation of a complex series of events, for instance.

CLASSIFYING WRITING SITUATIONS

The further question of how teachers' expectations are realised, or confounded, by the writing their pupils produce in response to their promptings is taken up later in this chapter. More closely related to the preceding discussion is the potential usefulness of a method for surveying all the occasions for writing a teacher may employ over a period of time. Ideally such a system should (*a*) offer a check list of the range and variety of situations devised, (*b*) call attention to possibilities left unexplored or choices over-used, (*c*) give the user evidence for identifying his individual style or pattern of preferences.

The category system which follows was improvised by the project group, after discussion and experiment, to meet these needs in finding patterns in the work we were studying.

A classification system for writing situations

(1a) Pictures, objects, events etc., used as the focus of attention throughout both preparation and writing.

(1b) Pictures, objects, events etc., used as an initial stimulus, but not subsequently recalled or stressed.

(2a) Children asked to focus on themselves and their own feelings in response to a situation.

(2b) Children asked to focus beyond themselves on an object or experience; an appeal to feelings minimal or absent.

(3a) Active physical participation by pupils in an experience before writing (e.g. going for a walk, exploring some aspects of the environment, improvised drama).

(3b) Mental participation; this will include discussion, anecdote, question and answer sequences, for example.

(3c) A purely passive role for pupils; this includes listening to exposition or instructions with writing following immediately.

(4a) Direct experience – a visit to a park, performing a science experiment.

(4b) Indirect experience – watching a film of a visit or a demonstration of an experiment on television.

(4c) Experience excluded – e.g. the teacher may explain in general terms what is required, but give no examples; one extreme form would be to offer a title for writing and nothing more.

(5a) Stimulus immediately present.

(5b) Past experience as the source of stimulation, even though an immediate stimulus may in some cases be used to prompt its recall.

(6a) Teacher as direct source of stimulus – reading a poem or story (i.e. interpreting as well as simply providing), painting a picture, carrying out some activity.

(6b) Children themselves as source – music making, drama as preliminary to writing, discussion in which the children actually provide the experience (through anecdote for example), a visit to, say, a speech festival in which the children were not solely spectators, but took part.

(6c) 'External' sources – book, film, film-strip, slide, tape-recording, record, television, radio, photographs, paintings, direct experience of environment (e.g. walking through fog); exploration of artefacts brought in, as opposed to those made by children or teacher.

(7a) Narrative – defined as a situation in which the emphasis is on treating a series of events in temporal sequence; this would usually be marked by labels such as 'story', 'account'.

(7b) Non-narrative.

(8a) Some direction of choice of syntactic structures for the opening sequence in writing; this may derive from the form of title given, from a common opening sentence or paragraph, from words and/ or phrases listed during a preparatory discussion.

(8b) No observable syntactic direction.

(9a) Primarily an aural stimulus (the various forms of discussion would be included here).

(9b) Primarily a visual stimulus.

(9c) Primarily a tactile stimulus.

Operation of the system is best shown by applying it to actual writing situations. The two examples that follow are consecutive instances from the full sequence provided by one of the project teachers. The descriptions are her own, transcribed from the records she supplied to us.

(1) 'Using voices and any handy thing suitable for producing appropriate sound effects, the class created a storm at sea. We tape-recorded the result! During the course of this operation, water was sloshed about in a pail (to get the sound of water lapping against the side of the boat). After the recording, I used the pail again, together with water poured from a jar and asked the class to find words to describe the sounds. We then went on to talk about "water" in the form of a raindrop, a river, the sea, a waterfall etc. The children then wrote stories, at my suggestion, evoked by this series of experiences. The tape was played a couple of times during the writing.'

The classification here would run – 1a (tape-recording heard during writing), probably 2a (experiencing a storm), 3a, 4a, 5a, 6a,b,c, 7a (because 'story' asked for), 8b, 9a. The implied purpose is expressive-poetic, audience (from knowledge of the teacher's way of working) the teacher as trusted adult and other children.

(2) 'Kevin brought his rabbit to school, which I allowed to roam freely round the room for fifteen minutes or so. The children were asked to observe her movements, the variety of her activities, what she felt like to the touch, the details of her appearance, the sounds she made. They talked to each other and exchanged ideas while this was going on. I then asked them to write as accurate a description as possible of her (she remained visible while the writing was going on, but no longer wandering about).'

Classification – 1a, 2b, 3a, 4a, 5a, 6c, 7b, 8b, 9a,b,c. Purpose is clearly expressive–transactional (report). Audience is not explicit, but likely to be similar to that in the first situation.

When descriptions like these for one term's writing collections (140 situations in all) were examined in this way, patterns of selection and emphasis emerged very vividly. Most teachers, unlike the one quoted above, were drawn to 1b in attempting to meet the requirement of creative writing. A tiny handful only set up situations for factual writing which fell into 1b. Some teachers showed a powerful and consistent preference for direct experience as a starting point, regardless of kind of writing aimed at; others used direct experience for factual, indirect for creative; a few made no use of direct experience at all. Surprisingly, only three of the 35 teachers involved in this collection made use of the recall of past experience (5b) to evoke creative or personal writing, where this might be thought to be the richest source of material. One persuasive explanation is that this is further evidence to support an earlier argument: an orthodoxy is produced to control new ways of working. Collecting bits of experience from the past is seen as a fact-finding operation, leading more or less inevitably to factual (report) writing. 'Imagination' or 'creativity' becomes associated with the immediate and novel. The value of a category like 'expressive' for writing is well illustrated here in helping to resolve this over-simplified opposition of terms.

Of equal importance is that the same experience may give rise to very different writing outcomes, according to the focus of attention suggested. The first example above could have been used to begin a series of projects on water, with transactional writing a natural product. The second, with a change of emphasis by the teacher, could have led to a flood of rivals to *Watership Down*.

THEMES AND VARIATIONS

In the days when 'essays' or 'compositions' were the staple of writing programmes in schools, advice on what to write about was an enviably straightforward affair. Textbooks would offer lists of titles or subjects, sometimes running to several hundred suggestions. If those proved insufficient, you were advised to study the subjects chosen by the eighteenth- and nineteenth-century essayists for inspiration, or, as a last resort, the leader columns of 'respectable' newspapers. That simplicity has vanished, and in its place the complex of interlocking concerns explored in Chapter 3 dominates any attempt to list or categorise topics or experiences to stimulate writing.

What is possible is a survey of those ideas, practices, inventions and rediscoveries in evoking children's writing that seem to justify themselves both by results and on the grounds of functional relevance. The distinction intended by this last proviso is no more than a restatement of an earlier plea: writing should be an integral part of the experience, achieving worthwhile ends. For this purpose, the act of writing is at least as significant as the finished result, particularly for the children we are considering. An American teacher, Roger Applebee (writing in *New Movements in the Study and Teaching of English*, edited by Nicholas Bagnall), saw this recognition as a notable mark of British teaching practices, by contrast with those in his own country: 'The ideal British teacher of English is inclined to think of writing as a natural, if not instinctive, activity for a young person. Writing becomes part of him and there is generally much more emphasis on the act itself than on the end product.'

No ideal organising principle suggests itself for controlling the extraordinary variety of situations that involve writing. What follows is divided into three sections, dealing with writing for self (which corresponds to Moffett's category of 'reflection', free of the demands of an external reader), writing for and with others (where the 'I–you' relationship becomes important) and using writing to deal with the world of events (where 'I – it' is the link to be established). The sections interpenetrate and overlap, but are not entirely without separate existences.

(1) *Writing for Self*

(a) *Diaries.* There was a time when sessions of 'news' exchanges were all the rage in infant classrooms, but they now seem much less common. One undoubted weakness was that they became routine without sensitive handling; another that 'news' tended to be interpreted, by the children at least, as nothing less than an apocalyptic event, to be invented if not experienced. A sense of competition was induced by public hearings and parents credited with astounding feats: 'My mum brought home a baby sister and a brother and some kittens and a budgie.' Yet this is in many ways the ideal foundation for the speech-writing transition, rooted firmly in experience and demonstrating the power of language to shape and fix understanding. The diary is a natural extension of 'news', but it is a private record of what matters to its writer. A teacher can give an initial impetus by example; a judicious selection of her own observations provides the incentive for children to see the familiar, the taken-for-granted, in a new way and to make that experience their own by recording it.

(b) *Commonplace Books, Personal Anthologies.* Taking a rather different route from the diary, these are complementary to diary-making in selecting, ordering and seeking to make sense of experience. Their contents need not, perhaps should not, be solely verbal, though language provides both commentary and structure. Photographs, drawings, cartoons, other artwork in variety, leaves, flowers will find a home here with extracts from favourite pieces of reading, experiments with writing and playing with language, anything that seems worth preserving.

(c) *Autobiographies.* A good deal of what emerges as 'creative' writing by juniors is of this form. Its connection with the preceding categories makes it worth encouraging for itself. Autobiography requires a further step for the writer in submitting to the demands of form; selection, emphasis and narrative sequence now become important. In addition, the sense of a possible outside reader becomes stronger, and worrying at the meanings of experiences more sustained. An extract from a 13-year-old's remembering indicates the possibilities:

'at the age of five I remember having a tug-of-war which happed to envolve a mouse which was dead and a stupid brother, we held the mouse after getting it out of the trap and had a fight over it and it ended in a tug of war and I ended up holding the skin of its tail my brother had got the body of it but another fight started and we decided to share it and so in the end we cut up the dead mouse and buried in two different place's to tell the truth I did not mind cutting up the mouse.'

Recent experiments with photography by young children suggest that this is a powerful method of inducing speaking and writing. As a starting point for autobiography it has obvious attractions in providing a complementary mode for capturing people, places, events.

(d) *Note-making*. Too often this skill seems to be taken for granted or ignored, with predictable results when complex project work is being attempted. Notes – to aid the memory, to capture a musing or speculation, to act as a running commentary on some activity, to provide the raw material for later reworking – should be talked about and practised so that this vital technique has a chance to become habitual.

(2) *Writing for and to Others*
(a) *Letters.* In many ways the most direct and readily understandable encounter with the concept of audience. Letters normally emerge from situations which demand their form, offer a clear purpose and a known recipient. Their fall from favour was undoubtedly contributed to by their use as exercises, addressed to imaginary pen-friends, fictional relatives or unlikely employers. Equally stultifying was the insistence of some teachers on the minutiae of presentation, accuracy in which, to the last comma, displaced all concern for the content. To match 'Dear Sir' with 'Yours sincerely' was a far more heinous crime than to compose a completely incomprehensible message.

Alvina Burrows, in *They All Want to Write*, argued convincingly from her work in American schools that natural occasions for simple letters arose even with very young children – invitations to parents to attend school activities, expressions of thanks to other children who had helped infants to carry out practical work, exchange with other classes and other schools.

With junior-school children, the possibilities expand, particularly in connection with project work. Not only may teachers involve their pupils in preparatory enquiries, but also in communicating the results to concerned outsiders and engaging in any ensuing dialogue. Ecological surveys, local history studies, exploration of the human environment benefit enormously from such exchanges, not least in asserting the usefulness of the undertaking for others. Necessarily, the teacher must be concerned to avoid being the instigator of those shoals of letters to major institutions which arouse justifiable impatience in their recipients. British Rail is not amused to receive requests for 'everything you know about railways'. The growth of project work and individualised learning at all educational levels needs to be protected from too much undirected zeal, if the full value of these methods is to be realised.

Whether there is any place in school for the writing of personal letters is very much open to argument. On balance it seems unlikely that the situation will arise naturally, unless teachers encourage exchanges on a personal level with other schools.

(b) *Summaries, Paraphrases.* These are perhaps as often written for oneself as for others, but they find a place in this category because of their importance in selecting and conveying information and understanding. Though related activities, they need different kinds of skill and children need to be helped to distinguish them. The evidence of an uncomfortably large bulk of topic or project work points to an almost total reliance on copying as a means of dealing with the written word. The value of such 'scissors-and-paste' compilations for enlarging understanding is probably negligible, but it seems to be a habit hard to break, once established.

Summary, the process of reducing the bulk of a communication without losing any of its essential features, is most readily encouraged at first in relation to narrative and in oral form. Retelling stories, heard or read, creates circumstances in which an interested and experienced audience of children readily comment on deficiencies in selection, sequence and emphasis. The process is, too, an important component in reviews (*see* (c) below).

Paraphrase, expressing the sense of a communication in different words, is a skill inevitably learnt in the process of learning language : if a listener misunderstands or fails to understand what you say, repetition alone is quickly discovered to have limited uses. Sustained written paraphrase is much less frequently needed and an elusive and difficult art to perform. Again, it must have a demonstrable function, a condition not met by requests addressed to students of all ages and conditions to 'put into your own words what the poem is about'. This is a comprehension exercise of a narrow kind which does considerable disservice to poetry, except when its concern is, for instance, to contrast the language structures employed in prose and poetry.

Two situations, at least, arise in junior schools where paraphrase is desirable and necessary. The first involves able (or older) children interpreting for the benefit of less able (or younger) pupils. Though this often occurs orally, there are occasions when the written form would be more useful – instructions for playing a game or carrying out a particular operation, for example, where printed instructions are too formal or too densely structured to be comprehensible. The second centres on the need to change one style for another and this is where the assault on copying can become most direct. The studiedly neutral, highly generalised style of many information texts in junior schools has to be worked on to make it fit the context it is needed for, if it is not to prove both alien and indigestible. 'The heat generated by this compression of the mixture is not sufficient to cause combustion, so sparking plugs are used to produce a spark which ignites the mixture and enables combustion to take place' (from a book on the working of internal-combustion engines, to be found in many junior school collections).

(c) *Reviews.* Even with the best organised of libraries, children need help in finding what will appeal to them. Classification systems, lists of recommendations, teacher intervention are only partial solutions. Building a series of commentaries by pupils on books provides a powerful and effective supplement. The dual function of review, to clarify the individual's own response and to advise and inform others, makes it well worth promoting. It includes, in brief compass, not only summary, but also reflection and judgement. No prescription of form is necessary, though painstakingly thorough accounts of narrative content need to be discouraged, if only to preserve the need for the reader to be driven on by wanting to know what happens next.

Other modes of experience, television programmes for instance, are in a different situation because, without a videotape recorder, they are not preserved for others to sample. Nevertheless, an agreement to watch a particular programme and to respond to it in discussion and writing is a potent way of extending and reshaping understanding.

(d) *Explanations, Commentaries, Instructions.* Many opportunities occur for employing language in these ways with practical benefits.

Much craft work involves finding solutions to problems of construction which then need laboriously to be rediscovered. A record of how a result was achieved, a blueprint for others to follow, produces the double reward, for its creators and those encouraged to follow their example. Here words and diagrams work together.

Commentaries are less specific in their concerns and may take a whole range of shapes. A title for a picture is a simple starting point, but this may develop into an explanatory note or further into reflective commentary. Thus Jane (aged 10) on a painting of the sea she had finished a week earlier: 'I don't like it now, though I did when I finished it. The colours are wrong but I was too lazy to mix different blues. The sailing boat is supposed to be in a storm but it looks like a toy in the bath. How do you paint clouds that look like clouds? The cliffs look real – perhaps I took more time doing them – but the waves are horrible. They don't have sharp edges like that.'

With a variety of machines and working models made by children in many classrooms, opportunities for producing clear operating instructions abound, again using pictures and words to achieve the most effective results. The need for clarity, attention to order and conciseness in this kind of communication is recommendation enough for its wider employment.

(3) *Writing and World of Events*

Though some of the kinds of writing of importance here have been treated in the foregoing sections, there is an argument for separate consideration of these situations which demand the recording or reporting of observations, the generating of hypotheses and a progress up the ladder of abstraction.

The extent and pace of change in teaching science and mathematics in junior schools in recent years forces a careful consideration of the new demands made on writing skills by these developments. Though the most obvious differences are those of content, giving substance to claims for the appearance of 'new' mathematics and 'new' science, there has been a significant shift of emphasis in the tasks required of children. An illustration from a popular mathematics textbook, Fletcher and Howell's *Mathematics for Schools* (1972), shows how central writing, in forms other than mathematical notation, has become in exploring and understanding the properties of numbers.

In the Teacher's Book for Level II, Book 5, page 19 contains the notes for beginning a study of statistics. Among the activities listed are (*a*) collection of data on the duration of specific kinds of television programmes; (*b*) recording personal behaviour over a period of 24 hours and, after recording the results on a bar chart, writing a 'white paper' on them (a descriptive, explanatory commentary); (*c*) writing an account of discoveries about the frequency of occurrence of letters in print, relating this to the length of Morse code symbols and the pattern of letters on a typewriter keyboard; (*d*) recording amounts of time spent on television for sport or comedy for each day of a week and discussing reasons for any variations.

In science, writing to record and explain has always been a major activity; what has particularly marked science off from other areas of the curriculum has been its association with a rigidly-defined form and style of writing and speaking. Clive Sutton, in his contribution to *The Art of the Science Teacher* (1974), describes the situation very neatly: 'It is often not the processes inside the test-tubes or circuits or leaves which are mysterious, *but the way of talking about them*', and further: '[Teachers] are still influenced by the idea that to write in the third person is somehow more scientific than to talk of "I" or "We".'

His recommendations for practice are in line with the suggestions made earlier for giving children the opportunity to find their way out of the expressive to fully-transactional forms of writing by exploration and experiment. He asserts that pupils must have used personal language for drawing conclusions before being asked to attempt them in impersonal forms. 'First writings in science should be at one extreme of the continuum from "writing for oneself" to "writing for others".' Of particular interest is his conclusion that the diary form is more important than the science report in these early stages of learning and that a stereotyped format should be avoided.

The vitally-necessary impersonal view of experience is not established at a sudden stroke. It emerges from the process of shedding personal elements; it takes time and has to be learnt and the junior school years are developmentally the right ones for beginning and consolidating that learning.

STARTING POINTS

An attempt to catalogue every conceivable occasion and subject for writing would be an absurdity, because it would involve listing everything in the natural world and in the infinite variety of worlds of the imagination and intellect. To bring together a selection of those ideas that have worked with young children is a more modest enterprise, for interpretation and use *within the setting provided by purpose and audience*. Without that last proviso, we are back to the sterility of composition titles whose sole purpose was to provide for the time labelled 'writing', with little thought for what was being accomplished, or why.

Nevertheless, most of us at some time need ideas to stimulate our own flagging imaginations or to alert us to possibilities not yet considered. Reference has been made earlier to a number of sources, among which Dora Pym's *Free Writing*, Margaret Langdon's *Let the Children Write* and Sir Alec Clegg's collection *The Excitement of Writing* stand out. To these may be added Margery Hourd's distinguished explorations of poetry writing, *The Education of the Poetic Spirit* and *Coming into Their Own* and Marie Peel's *Seeing to the Heart*. More eclectic surveys are represented by Barry Maybury's *Creative Writing for Juniors* and by Lane and Kemp's *An Approach to Creative Writing in the Primary School*. At least one usefully single-minded compendium of ideas has been published: T. G. Jeremiah's *A Source Book of Creative Themes*. Here eighty-seven themes are listed, ranging alphabetically from 'adventure' to 'zoos' with exhaustive cross-referencing of source material listed by kind: art, recorded sound, poetry, literature, reference books, films, film strips, charts. Most general books on the teaching of English in primary or junior schools have sections worth exploring on the starting points for writing; Geoffrey Roberts's *English in Primary Schools* will stand as helpfully representative of this category.

A guarantee of success with any idea for writing is an illusion, as all teachers will testify. What works for one teacher, with one class, in one set of circumstances might as well fail as prosper for another teacher in a similar, or totally different, situation. Some general, though still fallible, conclusions are possible on the manner of operation of some classes of stimuli simply from observing a wide range of situations in which they are used.

(1) *Objets Trouvés*

At one point in the mid-1960s, teachers, and more especially teachers in training, turned beachcombers and scoured Britain's beaches clear of driftwood. One or two of the remarkable shapes fashioned by the sea proved highly evocative for talk and writing; most did not. One image will stand to represent and in part to explain the failures: a slight but determined student dragging a 35-pound section of discarded railway sleeper more than two miles to a class of polite but puzzled 8-year-olds. Association value (since even its origin was unknown to both finder and class) nearly zero. Evocative, image-inducing objects are worth searching for, but they are rarer than we like to believe. Some fascinating possibilities in bones are offered by Peter Abbs in *Creating for Ourselves*, in his recent 'Approaches' series, where photographs stand in for the objects themselves.

(2) *Photographs*
Ever since Clements, Dixon and Stratta showed so convincingly the power of carefully-selected photographs to extend and illuminate a printed text (*Reflections*, 1963), their use in relation to writing has become commonplace. As with objects though, choice is a taxing and often frustrating business. Sydney Bolt reported entertainingly (in Chapter 2 of his *The Right Response*) on the written reactions of his further education students to one of the *Reflections* photographs, showing a policeman talking to a small boy. The same photograph shared with groups of second- and third-year juniors, inspired eager talk and varied writing; yet apparently equivalent images worked fitfully or not at all. From the experiences of these experiments and the evidence of the project, one significant feature is the extent to which interpretation is 'closed' or 'open'. There appears to be a necessary level of ambiguity for a photograph to succeed in arousing uniquely individual associations. Too much ambiguity and nothing happens; too little and the responses show little or no variation. With juniors, human interest seems to be if not essential then desirable, offering some opportunity for identifying with a person depicted.

(3) *Pictures*
Whether postcard or large reproductions, or originals, what has been said about photographs applies with equal force to pictures. One important extension, attested to by those project teachers who used the technique, is that process may be as valuable as product. Creating a picture (or a three-dimensional piece) with or without dialogue and running commentary, led to writing different in both kind and emphasis from that using a finished article as starting point. Sequences of pictures, photographs or cartoons offer a reliable basis for narrative writing with younger children.

(4) *Music*
In addition to the observations at the beginning of this chapter, one other general statement arises from the project writing situations. Too much of a piece can have a numbing effect as far as subsequent writing is concerned, though a limited exception needs to be made for music with narrative (e.g. *Peter and the Wolf*). Often a few bars will be enough (though the whole of the piece can and often should be enjoyed with the finished writing later).

(5) *Events*

Teachers whose experience goes back a few years will remember nostalgically a brief enthusiasm among their colleagues for striking matches or causing even more spectacular conflagrations as a preliminary to talk and writing. At another time bubble-blowing outfits were in short supply and 'iridescent' enjoyed a brief reign as a universal vogue word. The unusual and the unexpected are valuable ways of firing the imagination, of providing new directions for attention, but over-used and with too little concern for their purpose, they quickly degenerate into party tricks.

(6) *Objects*

The range of possibilities is very wide, with children and teacher contributing. Among those that achieved very obvious success with some of our group of children were: a Tibetan prayer wheel, a collection of hats, a pony's skull, a stuffed fox with one leg missing, a model stagecoach, a boomerang, a small nineteenth-century writing case with a hidden compartment. Since an even longer list could be compiled, from the same collection, of objects that failed to generate any enthusiasm, the key to success is likely to be located not in the objects themselves, but in the questions and comments encouraged in response to them. 'What is it?' needs to be supplemented by 'Where did it come from?', 'Who made it?', 'How did it get here?', 'Why was it made?', 'Who might have owned it?'

(7) *Literature*

Our teachers showed a marked and not unexpected preference for using poetry to fulfil some of the requests for creative writing, with prose (often the current class story) as a less frequent source. Only two teachers in the first collection and three in the last made use of children's poetry and narratives for this purpose; surprising in view of the range of anthologies available and the expectation that pupils might more readily become involved with the efforts of authors like themselves. None employed the children's own writing for this purpose, though Alvina Burrows argues persuasively for this procedure in *They All Want to Write*, and John Dixon asserted in *Growth through English* that, seriously treated, children's writing becomes 'the literature of the classroom'.

On choice of material it would be unwise to generalise, since the most unlikely of sources have been triumphantly successful for perceptive (or lucky) teachers. One recommendation worth considering is concisely expressed by Nancy Martin, contributing to *Children Using*

Language, edited by Jones and Mulford. Talking about the effects of using literature as the common experience from which writing stems she concludes: 'Literature is clearly of crucial importance, but perhaps it should not be too near to the children's writing in time, or too directly linked by the teacher to what they are about to write.'

The first of these two cautions has a relevance going beyond its attachment here to literature. Writing often comes most naturally and freely after the experience on which it feeds has had time to incubate, to become assimilated. A great temptation in the circumstances of school is to call for writing to tread on the heels of the experience. With younger and less able children in the junior school this practice makes sense, but even in these cases it does not need to be universal.

(8) *Broadcasting Media*

All the schools involved in our experiment possessed at least one television set and access to radio. The teachers working with us offered an expectedly broad spread of views on the value and use of these aids for their work in general and for stimulating writing in particular. The use of television for writing purposes outscored radio by 6:1 in the two collections (comprising eight occasions for writing) that were analysed in detail. With very few exceptions, programmes were selected for their provision of factual information and the writing required was dominantly factual rather than creative. On a number of occasions when the programme format was fictional, children were asked to select out the facts presented and to ignore the dramatic presentation. The example of 'a good story, but not much history', examined in Chapter 3, shows that there are more ways than one of achieving a desired end and what should determine choice is appropriateness and effectiveness for the pupils concerned.

The possibilities in television and radio seem, for these purposes, to be relatively little explored so far, but two modest ventures observed recently were successful enough to suggest further trials. One teacher tape-recorded snatches of three separate interviews with people protesting about threats to their environment (a road scheme, the extension of a rubbish tip, industrial pollution) and asked his 10-year-olds to write, rehearse and record their feelings on some issue they felt strongly about. Another, fortunate to have the use of a video-tape-recorder for a few days, presented her third-year juniors with an edition of *Magic Roundabout*, minus the sound, and encouraged them to form groups of three or four to create dialogue and commentary in the manner of Eric Thompson.

If there is a single, summarising proposition to be derived from this chapter, it might be that any of the myriad sources for writing is capable of giving rise to an excitingly varied range, in form and function, of writing outcomes. Some of this variation is within the teacher's control. We may suggest a way of responding to the experience, the preferred choice among the set of possible forms, direct the selection of content. Yet the difference between what we expect and what our pupils compose is often enough disconcertingly large.

We may look to the children themselves to account for part of this disparity. They do manage to misinterpret, mishear or ignore perfectly adequate instructions or suggestions. The power of association is strong, too. After a class had engaged in making butter, they were asked to explain the process. One boy started in this direction, but was then drawn into reminiscence of the time he lost some butter he had been sent to buy. Sometimes the initial stimulus is insufficiently arresting to sustain interest for long, but the conscientious child will write on, though feeling no obligation to keep company with the original theme.

A closer look at those occasions in project writing where intention and outcome failed to match suggested that teachers had to shoulder much of the responsibility. Substituting one word for another, though apparently a trivial change, may profoundly affect the way a child interprets the task – 'Describe what you saw as you walked through the fog' gave very different results from 'Describe what you felt as you walked through the fog'. A similar effect is caused by the change from 'What does this music make you think of?' to 'What does this music make you feel?' Another part of the explanation lies with the degree of explicitness of instructions and suggestions for writing, set against the teacher's expectation. Instructions are as likely to cause confusion by being too detailed as by being too vague and the less expert the writers, the more likely this is to be true.

A complete resolution of this difficulty is impossible and ultimately undesirable; one of the great rewards in reading what children write is to see them discovering possibilities we were unaware of. In providing contexts for writing, we need to work for a creative tension between the provision of this valuable freedom and a considered progression to promote the skill and art of writing in the most effective way possible. Good ideas for writing are only the beginning. We must try to anticipate what they might give rise to and the most direct method is to write from them ourselves, at the stage of preparation and, more influentially, simultaneously with pupils. This, and other advantages of participating in writing, are convincingly attested to by the teachers quoted in Stratta, Dixon and Wilkinson's *Patterns of Language*. The workshop approach to in-service teacher education should help to banish our fears of this kind of public, shared performance and our audience is, after all, tolerant, tactful and kindly disposed towards our efforts.

Janet (fourth-year junior) – 'Mr H. wrote a poem with us yesterday and read it out. I liked the title very much.'

6
Towards a Programme for Writing

'Improvisation can thrive only within a framework that expresses, more or less articulately, an underlying pattern of development . . . What we want is something less specific than a curriculum and more ordered than chaos.'
(John Dixon – *Growth through English*)

'That problem is to direct pupils' oral and written speech, used primarily for practical and social ends, so that gradually it shall become a conscious tool of conveying knowledge and assisting thought.'
(John Dewey – *How We Think*)

In devising a syllabus or, more modestly, a scheme of work for a class, a teacher is constrained to answer a number of questions before the process can begin. What experience, skills, understanding do the pupils possess for whom the work is intended? What are the expected outcomes? What methods, techniques, resources are available for carrying through the process and which are likely to prove most profitable? What are the characteristics of what is to be taught? The answers to the first three of these questions are readily accessible in all but the rarest of cases, though there may well be uncertainty about the best method or the most useful range of resources if a new departure is planned. With the fourth question, the element of uncertainty becomes more prominent, varying with the special properties of the subject discipline concerned and what is known about how it is learned.

The teacher of mathematics, confronted by the need to take children on from the stage of simple counting, is aware that the next logical operations are addition and subtraction, with multiplication and division some way on, to be tackled after these earlier understandings have been established and explored. In this sense mathematics is a highly-structured subject; there is agreement not only on its content, but, with relatively minor exceptions, on the order and progression of elements within it. Arithmetic precedes algebra, whole numbers are encountered before fractions.

English, by contrast, has often been called the subject without content, especially after the stage of initial skill mastery. A vast body of information exists on the initial teaching of reading, though disagreement among theorists and practitioners on choice of method and medium has contrived to conceal the extent of fundamental agreement on what is involved. The Bullock Committee, in its report, *A Language for Life*, starts its chapter on the reading process by reaffirming this view:

'Let us, therefore, express our conclusion at the outset in plain terms: there is no one method, medium, approach, device or philosophy that holds the key to the process of learning to read. We believe that the knowledge does exist to improve the teaching of reading, but that it does not lie in the triumphant discovery, or rediscovery, of a particular formula. Simple endorsements of one or another nostrum are no service to the teaching of reading' (paragraph 6.1).

The nature and importance of reading has assured it of the close and continuing attention necessary to accumulate that knowledge. Other aspects of literacy have been less assiduously served. The point was made in an earlier chapter that the formal teaching of language rested for more than a century on a grammatical description in many ways inappropriate for its purpose. Nor was it only content that was deficient. The order of items for teaching was traditional and largely unquestioned. An 1814 textbook, *The Young Man's Companion*, defined the appropriate sequence for learning as orthography, etymology (which included functions as well as the derivation of words), syntax, prosody. With due allowance made for changes in labels over the ensuing century-and-a-half, that sequence is still recognisable in primary and secondary English textbooks of our own time. The underlying proposition is plain enough: proceed from the smallest units upward, on the assumption that small equals simple. Yet grammar at the level of 'word' is no less complex than the grammar of 'sentence'. In Chapter 4 the evidence from our writers indicated an approach to mastery of clause use before an understanding and use of functionally-equivalent phrases. The system, however, has invariably treated phrases before clauses for teaching purposes.

All this is by way of a justification for what might seem the exaggerated caution of this chapter's title. Why not simply 'a programme (or syllabus, or policy) for writing'? Part of the answer derives from the parallels, just illustrated, in other areas of language activity. In the case of writing, as for these others, there is a pressing need to appraise all the available evidence, to sift out opinion, assertion, unexamined traditional practices, and work on what is left. Such has been writing's position in the educational process that this exploration reveals a surprising number of unanswered questions. The close relationship with reading has ensured that the first stages of writing, those concerned with the technical skill of making recognisable marks and assembling them into conventional units, are well documented and uncontroversial. True, from time to time arguments break out over the relative merits of different handwriting styles, but they leave untouched the fundamental agreement on the content and order of early writing activities. At the stage of adolescent progress in writing towards adult maturity another concentration of attention occurs. A glance at an extensive bibliography of enquiries into writing, such as Braddock, Lloyd-Jones and Schoer's *Research in Written Composition*, amply confirms this emphasis.

Between these two extremes, enquiry has been much more spasmodic, though interest in the end-products, in the form of anthologies, is manifestly high. An instructive comparison is possible with reading: what have come to be known variously as the 'intermediate' or 'higher' skills of reading have been left largely to look after themselves until quite recently. For writing, once the technical skill was established, practice was assumed to be enough. 'Writing is learnt by writing' is an unarguable but only partial truth. What it omits acted as a focus for the enquiry from which this book takes its origin, though that work has no pretensions to making good all, or even most, of the omissions. With all that has emerged in recent years on the nature of writing and its development in children, the firmly-plotted landmarks are still widely separated, the map of the area still in process of being transformed from medieval to modern.

Thus far, one justification for caution. The other refers to a recurring theme in what has gone before; development is a uniquely individual process in which no two children follow exactly the same line. Though some general similarities appear, it would be folly to forget that they express only part of the story. To treat them as a complete, unvarying description of how all children advance in skill and range is to invite a return to the strait-jacketed prescription so justly condemned in earlier teaching, with its accompanying apparatus of graded exercises and purposeless writing activities. Once again *A Language for Life* provides a summarising comment: 'The difficulty of structuring development in writing, whether in English or in other subjects, has too often been regarded as insuperable, or as likely to lead to mechanical exercises and practices. There has not been enough thought given to the different varieties of English and to the stages of language development at which children can begin to cope with them' (paragraph 11.6).

What this chapter seeks to do, then, is to bring together the evidence on which such structuring or planning may be based, with the intention of offering to teachers a set of propositions out of which they are free to fashion their own versions, for writing, of 'something less specific than a curriculum and more ordered than chaos'.

A SURVEY OF EVIDENCE

(1) *Cognitive development.* A number of choices is available for descriptions of how a child's intellectual processes advance from infancy onwards, but perhaps the most persuasive and complete is found in the work of the Swiss psychologist, Jean Piaget. Over the past fifty years the elaborations of his theory have helped bring about a fundamental change in our understanding of the child's view of the world and forced a continuing re-examination of educational practice. It is a qualitatively different world from the adult's, because a child's mental structure is different. The best known example is probably that of conservation, where some of Piaget's experiments are both simply performed and startling in their implications. Young children (in Piaget's terms, those at a pre-operational stage of development) deny conservation. Faced with two identical balls of plasticine and observing one being rolled out into a sausage shape, a child at this stage will assert that the amount of substance has been changed. A similar phenomenon is demonstrable with continuous quantities (liquids poured into containers of a different shape from the original), number, weight, volume.

This is one illustration of the proposition that a child has to learn to deal with properties of experience and, during this process, passes through a series of recognisable stages in cognitive development. The importance of these stages for the junior school teacher is that three of them are relevant for her children. Without entering into the complexities of the argument between Piagetians and their critics over the propriety of relating these stages to age, there is ample evidence to show that, between seven and eleven, children will demonstrate in their thinking signs of what Piaget called pre-operational, concrete operational and formal operational thought. Operations may be defined as internalised actions which have the property of being reversible. Thus a child in the experiment with plasticine who accepts that the quantity has not changed will have grasped that the action can be reversed: what is rolled out can be rolled back up again. This is the level of concrete operations, where the experience is immediately present. The final stage, in Piaget's theory associated with adolescence, is that of formal operations, where thinking is dominated by the formation of hypotheses and is not bound by what is observed.

The full implications of Piaget's theory for teaching and learning extend well beyond the immediate concerns of this chapter and need closer attention than is possible here. (A concise and clear account is given in Ginsburg and Opper's *Piaget's Theory of Intellectual Development*.) Those ideas which shape practice and have relevance for writing are not easily summarised but include:

(a) no generalisation from an adult's experience to a child's is altogether safe. A logical arrangement of material may be unhelpful or confusing for a child; what is self-evident to a 16-year-old may be a mystery to his 10-year-old brother;

(b) the teacher must become, above all else, a sensitive observer and interpreter of his pupils' actions, striving to gain insight into the current level of intellectual functioning of each of them;

(c) children at these early stages learn best from a wide variety of concrete activities; verbal understanding is a later development. The teacher's job is not to transmit facts or concepts, but to promote active physical and mental exploration by providing appropriate opportunities.

(2) *Social development.* Piaget describes a matching process of movement towards maturity in the way a child sees himself in relation to the world about him. From a position of egocentricism, where only his own point of view has meaning, he emerges first into a stage of incipient cooperation, and then to genuine co-operation, as he gradually learns to understand the position of other people and to view experience from more than a fixed point.

(3) *Language.* The evidence explored in detail in Chapter 4 does not need to be repeated here, but one general characteristic of language development in writing during these junior-school years is worth re-iterating. This is the conclusion on the variation in the rate of development, reproduced, from our enquiry, in *A Language for Life* (paragraph 11.23): 'The advance towards linguistic maturity is modest but steady over the first Junior school year, quickening somewhat in the second year, accelerating markedly in the third and slowing to something like the first year pace in the fourth.'

One related theme, again associated with Piaget and particularly with the egocentric phase of development, is the nature of the link between thinking and language. Young children employ speech to and for themselves, producing a running commentary on their activities, requiring neither audience nor reply. For Piaget this egocentric speech gradually gives way to mature, socialised speech as the child escapes from the limitation of his own viewpoint. Vygotsky persuaded Piaget that there was a more convincing explanation of this change; the monologue, with its function of assisting activity and organising experience, was too important to be simply replaced. He argued that it gradually becomes internalised as 'inner speech', normally by the age of seven or so, and only comes to the surface in circumstances of difficulty or stress. Most adults will be able to supply personal examples of being driven to 'think out loud', often in struggling to solve an unfamiliar problem.

The coincidence of this internalisation of speech with the effort to master the complexities of reading and writing and with the period of transition from pre-operational to concrete-operational thinking directs attention very forcefully at the importance, for learning, of experience in the first junior-school year. There is a reminder of what was said earlier about the need to establish confidence in the expressive mode of language before encouraging extensive exploration from that base.

SUGGESTIONS FOR PROGRESSIONS IN WRITING

James Moffett, in *Teaching the Universe of Discourse*, provides an apt link between the general world of the child growing up and the effort to reflect this understanding in helping writing to develop. He opens his second chapter with the declaration: 'The most sensible strategy for determining a proper learning order in English, it seems to me, is to look for the main lines of child development and to assimilate to them, when fitting, the various formulations that scholars make about language and literature.'

This section is concerned with exemplifying some 'proper learning orders' for writing and commenting on them, though there are few in anything like the developed form that Moffett devises; another indication that writing has been left to take care of itself in this respect.

(1) *Beginnings.* Though the very first stage in mastering the physical skill of writing is outside the scope of this book, some reference to it is necessary, if only because a significant minority of children appear in the junior school as non-writers or very uncertain in their grasp of the process. Essential in these first encounters, as later, is that children are helped to see the purpose of the activity, as well as its components. The closer the association between writing and reading, deliberately promoted, the easier these requirements are to satisfy. One strength of

the *Breakthrough to Literacy* materials, produced by Mackay and Thompson, is this strong association: a child composes writing, which in turn becomes his reading and then a model for true writing. Since what he composes is from his own language resources, to meet his immediate interests, there is no problem of motivation or of appropriateness.

Ideas for pre-writing activities and the transition to technical control are well treated in a number of books concerned with literacy in the first school. Since there is a large measure of agreement on what is most effective, no summary is required here: a balanced and economic description of possibilities is provided by Joy Taylor in *Reading and Writing in the First School.* Her insistence on helping the learner to understand the purpose of the activity from the very beginning usefully echoes a major theme of this book: 'It is far more profitable for the child to be given, once in a few days, enough of the teacher's time to assemble his own writing really constructively, than to have a sentence hastily written for him every day, purporting to transcribe his own words but in fact amounting to little else than just something more for him to copy.'

Taking into account the powerfully egocentric view of most children at this stage it is their language that needs setting down, not a translation. Better 'I painted this Red Indian village', signed by John, than 'This is a Red Indian village' or 'John painted this Red Indian village'.

(2) *Early themes.* There is a remarkable consensus among many of those who have written about language work in the junior school on starting with exploration of the senses. Maybury, Lane and Kemp, Tucker (*Teaching English in the Middle Years*), Gregson (*English-Schooling in the Middle Years*) all have extensive and detailed suggestions for basing much speech and writing on these primary experiences. Since all our information on the world is collected by them, the agreement is perhaps not so remarkable after all. To use the senses as starting points is to meet the requirements of some general truths of teaching; begin with the child's own experience and understanding, prefer present to absent, concrete to abstract, look for the most direct and accessible ways of enlarging experience.

Within this general agreement, variations in order and emphasis appear. Some would argue that the most beneficial sequence is from the general to the particular, macro- to microcosm. Use the sense of sight first to scan a wood, then a tree, then a leaf. Others prefer a reverse order and this seems to accord better with what we know of children's intellectual processes at this stage.

In an earlier series of experiments, I investigated the range and depth of response in writing by junior children to sensory experiences. A consistent order emerged: the greatest fluency and variety was evoked by sight, followed by sound, then touch, taste, smell. Since this matches their relative importance in our lives, there is nothing startling in this, but it does warn of the difficulty involved in feeling satisfied with work derived from the last three, by comparison with sight and sound.

In employing sensory exploration as a shaping force for speaking and writing, care needs to be taken that the range of kinds is not unduly compressed. Much of this experiencing lends itself to a response in the form of a personal report – expressive writing moving towards transactional or even poetic. Adrian's piece reflects this general model.

Colours in my mind

'When I close my eyes gently, I see red, white and blue,
When I close my eyes tightly, I see dark green and black.
I see lakes of colours in my mind. Red, blue, white and all the others too.'

By moving the emphasis to the properties of seeing (e.g. the effects of using one eye only) a different kind of language response is suggested. Introducing the experience of others in seeing or not seeing allows another change of perspective and yet another kind of writing, reinforcing the process of learning to stand in another's shoes.

(3) *Topics, centres of interest, projects.* The importance and widespread use of these methods for organising learning make inevitable some attempt to analyse how the writing activities they generate may be related to a general writing programme. The selection and ordering of topics through the junior-school years are themselves interesting problems, but in most respects outside the scope of this discussion. Peter Rance, in *Teaching by Topics*, offers some well-considered solutions to those questions, but the balance of language activity is only incidentally treated.

Reference was made in the previous chapter to one unfortunate effect of narrowly-based enquiry: extensive and unreflective copying becomes the dominant and sometimes the sole language activity. The danger of this occurring clearly increases as the topic for exploration becomes less accessible to direct investigation by children, so that information is necessarily second-hand. This suggests strongly an order starting from immediately-present experience, extending in time and space only when our pupils are capable of making this borrowed information their own. Developing skill in paraphrase and summary, a general case argued in Chapter 5, is a priority in first- and second-year work. Matching texts to readers is equally important: we ask the impossible if children are confronted by writing whose level of abstraction is far removed from their modes of thinking. Though information books have improved enormously in recent years, notably in physical attractiveness, range and variety, their concern for appropriate language is still fitful and often misguided, relying on 'controlled' vocabulary and a firm belief in the virtues of the simple sentence.

The proper and effective use of quotation should be explored after the paraphrase and summary experiments are under way and contribute to their development. If a child, understanding a proposition in a book, sees that it is well expressed, he will be disconcerted by the general rule that everything must be translated into his own words. Again, the point of growth in understanding is to begin with a professional procedure: from the earliest attempts at note-making, encourage the listing of source. For direct quotations, whether at the information gathering stage or in the finished report or record, insist on title, author *and* page as accompaniment. Those few teachers in our group who used this technique claimed (and their evidence was convincing) that, among other benefits, there was a sharp reduction in indiscriminate copying.

Two further points are worth making about this source of writing. The first is the recurring theme of variety in kinds. The pressure is strong to expect impersonal writing, recording, reporting, informing and little else. Other uses of language should be built in, particularly as children consolidate their skills in these basic kinds and are ready for experiment. The beginnings of persuasion, speculation, argument are certainly possible by the third year, for more children than we suspect. Personal and imaginative writing demand admission too. The 'categories of writing' system described in Chapter 5 could be employed, with a language use analysis like that suggested by Eric Ashworth in *Language in the Junior School* (in Chapter 6, 'Language in Group Projects'), as a safeguard against too narrow a selection from among all the possibilities.

The final comment concerns the difficulty that teachers find in responding with enthusiasm to much of the writing that originates in project work. The contrast with 'creative' writing is marked and has undesirable consequences. One such is the use of 'factual' writing as the focus for work on technical problems with language, a practice regarded as improper with imaginative pieces. The balance needs redressing; the developing mastery of impersonal writing needs at least as much praise and encouragement as the other kind and informed, judicious criticism too, especially from the third junior year onward. As with imaginative writing, we need to develop ways of responding and these are likely to be best learnt from inside, trying these ways of shaping experience for ourselves.

(4) *Functional analysis.* The examination, in Chapter 3, of James Britton's function categories included some reference to the pattern of development associated with them. A young child's speech is expressive, with meanings rarely made explicit, because he finds it more or less impossible to escape from his egocentric position. Events *as he sees them* are the only reality and he cannot imagine any other position. Movement out of the expressive, as the child's world enlarges and meanings are required to be more explicit, is a relatively slow process, but one which most children will be embarked on by the time they reach the junior school.

In providing the settings in which these experiments with language are challenged to occur, teachers have to take separate account of the two available directions. For transactional writing, the key features are audience and purpose. When the audience for speech or writing cannot be expected to understand implicit meanings, pressure is exerted to find ways of meeting that audience's expectations. As purpose is directed outwards, to getting things done, the expressive mode shows its limitations. Confidence in producing expressive writing is a necessary prerequisite to these early experiments with new forms and is never replaced, but reinforced.

In the advance to the poetic function, language itself is at the centre of attention and its changing role needs to be savoured. Tom Haggitt, in *Working with Language*, summarised the teacher's task neatly: 'children should be encouraged to splash about with language'. Language games and language in games (the world explored so vividly by the Opies), beliefs about words and their power, sound and sense, all meet the criterion of deriving from children's immediate experience and they point towards the valuing of language for its own sake.

Providing contexts for writing, suggesting variations in purpose and audience are only part of the teacher's contribution; at least as important is the introduction of appropriate models of writing and helping children to discover and talk about significant features in what they produce. John and Kevin, whose science observations were quoted in Chapter 3, would not be helped by direct instruction on scientific methods of recording events, nor by the example of impersonal scientific writing. Their need is to discuss their recordings to see ways of extending the range and detail of their observations. Later they will be ready for the first moves away from the particular to the general and later still to the process of hypothesis making. Only by sensitive reading of their work will we be able to judge when the time is ripe to aid each step forward and what form that assistance should take. Equally our eagerness to provide opportunities for practice and experiment should not contribute to a deterioration of writing into routine performance. Poetic writing is, in a sense, its own justification, but transactional writing demands a clear purpose and a real audience.

A potentially valuable supplement to this development analysis is offered by the suggestion of Doughty, Pearce and Thornton in *Exploring Language* of four stages in the growth of language competence: recognition, familiarisation, hesitant command, fluent command. To be able to place a piece of writing accurately in this sequence is to indicate appropriate action. They argue, for instance, that the transition from hesitant to fluent command is most effectively accomplished by thorough preparation (going beyond the mere assemblage of material into discussion and reflection), extended practice and reworking of drafts until a final form is reached. Arguments over this 'workshop' approach to writing are examined in the next chapter: the issue here is the designation of stages and the help they may afford to the teacher in planning writing activities.

(5) *The Dartmouth progressions.* Contributors to the Anglo-American seminar at Dartmouth College, New Hampshire, in 1966 produced a number of tentative suggestions on lines of growth in language development, reported by John Dixon in *Growth through English*. Some of these have clear affinities with those already discussed, but they have a coherence which forbids fragmented listing.

(a) In using language a child moves from immediate and present experience, to what is coming next, to the past, and finally to potential rather than actual experience. The path is from the realm of events to that of logical possibilities.

(b) In telling and writing stories, children are able to use language to represent things in general, rather than the particular; to move towards a universalising of experience.

(c) Children begin their story making by projecting into the remote third person, and develop by stages towards a concern for the here-and-now, casting themselves in the role of participant.

(d) With increasing experience children become capable of setting down explicitly some of the meanings implicit in language and gesture.

(e) From a starting point in a limited, immediate and familiar audience, children learn to speak to distant and unfamiliar listeners or readers. The egocentric monologue is the base for creating an understanding of the large, unknown audience for formal writing.

(f) From using language about people and things, children develop gradually the powerful tool of using language about language.

(6) *Points-of-view and levels of abstraction.* This section began with a reference to Moffett's 'proper learning orders' and, logically enough, ends with a summary of his key propositions, particularly those that bear most directly on writing in the junior-school years. This does no sort of justice to his book: *Teaching the Universe of Discourse* has too distinctive a flavour to be sampled solely at pallid second-hand.

(a) A curriculum should be based on the hierarchy of abstraction, the process by which we select and order experience in order to understand it. The educational process begins with consciousness of abstraction; in this way we learn to rethink and unthink.
(b) The hierarchy of abstraction moves from the chronologic (narrative) through the analogic (generalising and classifying) to the tautologic (transforming propositions).

Readers will recognise the relationship between this progression and that of the transactional sub-classes in Britton's scheme, outlined in Chapter 3.
(c) In terms of distance between writer and subject, this order corresponds to what is happening, what has happened, what happened, what was happening, what happens (the analogic stage), what may happen (tautologic).
(d) These kinds of discourse may all be realised in each of the four speaker-audience relations: reflection, conversation, correspondence, publication (terms whose meaning was discussed in Chapter 3).

This presentation is itself at a high level of generality, analogic in its concern for classifying and creating propositions. Let us retreat from abstractions to concrete examples and relate the scheme to what children actually do, and select narrative fiction for its pervasiveness in writing.

Early in their lives, children become acquainted with the form; bed-time stories and nursery rhymes confirm real-life experience of events happening in chronological sequence. They are distant in time and space, told from the point of view of an omniscient narrator. The legends and fantasies which displace them as children grow older gradually reduce that distance and engage the narrator more and more in the action until the transition is possible to the here-and-now of naturalistic fiction at the end of the junior-school years.

This progress, responding to the underlying needs and understanding of the child, produces a parallel in writing. The movement is from remote 'no-person', through variants of third-person, to first-person narrative. This final change is clearly reflected in the language analysis, where the balance of personal pronoun preference crosses from 'he' to 'I' for most children early in the third year. However, the argument on egocentricity of point of view ensures that the *reverse* order is true when the child is dealing with realities and not fiction. Here the auto-biographical dominates the first stages of narrative reporting and pro-gress is measured by the gradual shedding of personal elements. Plan-ning for narrative over these years then involves two complementary processes. An outline scheme might look something like this:

	Fiction	*Fact*
1st year	remote subjects, modelled on reading – fantasy, legend, folk stories	autobiography, diary, first-person reporting
2nd year	historical themes following on towards end of year-reading to reflect different narrator positions (from de-tached to involved in action); trying on other identities	continue above, add letters, recording, first stages of summary, paraphrase
3rd year	encourage change from third- to first-person narra-tive; from historical fiction to 'eye-witness' position. Match with reading under-taken. Begin change to fiction set in own times	detached autobiography, leading on to first steps in biography, joint-reporting of project discoveries. Begin-ning the move out in space as well as time – assimilation of remote experience
4th year	contemporary themes, in-cluding ventures into time future – autobiographical fiction, with variations in narrator identity	extension and consolidation of third-year work. Where appropriate a beginning with speculation, argument. In-tensify concern with order, selection, emphasis. Im-aginative transference to narrate from other point of view.

The skeletal nature of the outline is deliberate; this is a speculation for experiment, not a detailed blueprint for action. It makes no provision for links with non-narrative writing and presumes an equivalence of experience, background and interest in children, together with an assumption of orderly development which would fit no group of children ever assembled anywhere. Nevertheless, it does have a foundation in how real children behave and taken together with the more general outlines that precede it, should furnish a series of reference points for planning individual writing policies or programmes. That evidence from such diverse sources suggests constancies in development is an encouragement for the belief that teachers can offer more than just practice in writing. They can begin to provide confident answers to the questions posed by Dewey and Dixon with which this chapter opened.

7

The Treatment of Writing

'We believe that extensive reading and writing are of prime importance for language growth but that they should be supported by explicit instruction. We cannot accept that the development of language can be left to chance, on the principle that "a relevant moment" will occur.'
(*A Language for Life*, paragraph 11.21)

'I can see that it is true of some skills that the ability to bring awareness of modes of operation to bear increases the degree of skill. I think this is much less true of language than of any other skill we deal with in school.'
(James Britton in Evertts's – *Explorations in Children's Writing*)

'If we were more aware of its [language's] imperfections, of the many ways in which it does not fit the universe it attempts to describe, of the paradoxes and contradictions built into it, then we could warn the children, help them see where words and experiences did not fit together, and perhaps show them ways of using language that would to some extent rise above its limitations.'
(John Holt – *How Children Fail*)

Hidden in the headword of this chapter's title is a necessary ambiguity. 'Treatment' is being made to serve its obvious purpose of referring to a set of procedures to which some existing object is subjected. For writing, this incorporates all those activities of responding to the finished piece which, in schools at least, have been dominated by appraisal, assessment, marking. This is treatment of outcome. At least as important is concern with process; all those antecedent circumstances that bear on what is finally produced. In this case 'treatment' refers to the variety of beliefs and aims which condition the activities preceding writing and the act itself: preparation for writing and the setting in which it happens.

No one will be surprised to learn that on these topics, as with so much else in teaching, diametrically-opposed solutions are commonplace. The quotations that introduce this chapter are representative of a much larger set that might have been used to show both large and subtle variations of view on the place of teaching about language. As with those used at the head of Chapter 4, exact comparisons are unwise and simple conclusions erroneous: to say of the Bullock Committee and John Holt that they are 'for' language teaching, while Professor Britton is 'against' would be to overlook vital distinctions in what they are talking about. The Bullock assertion focuses on the learner, while Holt and Britton are more concerned with the nature of language and how it works. Britton minimises the value of studying abstract linguistic principles as a means of increasing practical skill; Holt's attention is on the fallibility of language as an instrument and the need to understand how and why this is true.

What follows is an attempt to present and suggest ways of resolving these and other arguments and oppositions on principles and practices. For convenience, the two senses of 'treatment' are employed to create two distinct sections, though the total act of writing is an indivisible whole.

CONDITIONS FOR WRITING

Handwriting

To start with the basic skill of making appropriate marks on paper is immediately to become involved in matters where feelings have run high, and still do on occasions. There is little controversy about the general nature of pre-writing activities, directed at achieving left–right orientation and a sufficient degree of fine muscular control to permit reasonable accuracy in tracing paths and reproducing shapes. Most teachers, too, agree closely on materials and instruments for these early experiments; good-sized unlined paper and crayons, soft-lead pencils and felt-tip pens of sufficient substance to allow small hands a firm hold. The correct grip and posture are habits to be started from the outset and the special problems of left-handed writers, discussed in general terms in Chapter 4, given close attention.

Arguments tend to settle about two major concerns: choice of alphabet and provision for practice, with minor skirmishes over the choice of writing instruments. At the earliest stage the choice of alphabet rests essentially between print script and some form of modified cursive, such as the Marion Richardson script. Choice of the former is usually supported by reference to (a) the need to establish individual letter shapes firmly and (b) the similarity of this script to the print alphabet of first reading books. Selection of the cursive is normally justified on the grounds of economy of effort, with just one form to learn, not two, and that related to the need to develop an effective running hand.

If what is to be taught in these early years is to be a significant life-time gift, then this choice is one deserving serious attention. Three essentials of handwriting must be served: legibility, fluency, indi-viduality. The last two are ill-served by too lengthy an apprenticeship in print script. The Marion Richardson alphabet is rightly popular for its utility, but its forms make the development of an individual style a matter of some difficulty. Italic script has convinced and persuasive advocates for its use in junior schools and there is no denying the range of individual variations it permits. Nevertheless, for all its aesthetic qualities, it does pose problems of legibility and occasionally of fluency. My own preference is for the solution proposed by V. E. C. Gordon and R. Mock (in *Twentieth Century Handwriting*) for a cursive script de-rived from nineteenth-century round hand. This has fewer prohibitions of loops than the Marion Richardson style and seems better adapted to modification into an individually mature hand, while retaining ease of letter formation.

Table 59 in *A Language for Life* summarises the extent of hand-writing activities reported by the 936 schools sampled for their 6- and 9-year-old pupils. Twelve per cent of the younger children and 21 per cent of the older group had no time allocated for handwriting at all. In most schools at both ages, class-based work occupied at most thirty minutes a week and only 20 per cent of children were encouraged to practise handwriting in optional time, with again a practical limit of thirty minutes in any week. If a confident, fluent hand is to develop, opportunities for methodical instruction and practice must be found and a total of thirty minutes a week seems an irreducible minimum. This need not be seen as a road back to the miseries of the copy book; children can be encouraged to experiment with different kinds and qualities of paper, using as wide a variety of writing instruments as the school's allowance and the teacher's ingenuity can provide. To see many older secondary school pupils still painfully driving their pens with their tongues is to realise the need for this habitual skill to be established early and thoroughly.

Language Study

Evidence that the formal study of a language, particularly its grammar, has no measurable effect on the ability to write has been steadily ac-cumulated throughout this century, but the belief still lingers on that it somehow *must* be beneficial. Textbooks, with their methodical exer-cises, still abound and, where they have been supplanted, work cards are devised which mirror in content and technique their predecessors. *A Language for Life* (paragraph 11.20) reports: 'In our visits to schools we found that the teaching of language through weekly exercises was still commonly to be found at all age levels, but particularly in the primary school.'

This is not a prelude to a conclusion that language study is worthless and should be instantly dismissed from all classrooms. A delight in, and understanding of, language and its workings is a vital component of good speaking and listening, reading and writing. What is at issue is how these ends are best served and the answer is likely to lie in the content of language study and the setting it is given, directly related to the needs and developmental situation of individual children.

To separate the study of language from its use is to cut children off from their own expertise and to make advances in mastery most difficult. As W. O'Donnell puts it in *Applied Linguistics and the Teaching of English*: 'In acquiring grammar for use, that is to say, the human mind operates most efficiently on language – not by studying language about language.' We do not go about the business of extending our vocabulary by systematically reading a dictionary. The assimilation of new words starts from need; the need to understand what others are saying to us and to make our meanings clear to them. There is no practical virtue for the language user to be able to assign grammatical labels to his language, for classification's sake alone. Yet these assumptions were the basis for the vocabulary exercises, parsing and analysis of yesterday and continue to act as justification for today's language work. Children need an understanding of the structures of language and their functions, but in the context of use, when a problem of communication needs a solution.

A series of negative injunctions is easily enough collected and perhaps agreed to, but they are not much help in suggesting a way forward for teachers concerned more for what should be tried than avoided. The propositions which follow are intended to serve as a necessarily limited set of reference points from which the individual teacher can begin to shape experiments for his own situation:

(1) Knowing about language and about writing should be high priorities in preparing for teaching. This is no more than an endorsement of the arguments in Chapters 23 and 24 of the Bullock Report for the importance of language study in initial and in-service teacher education. The production of professional grammarians is not intended, but the concerns of many branches of linguistic study bear directly on the content and aims of teaching, though, as has been

admitted earlier, solutions to all practical problems are still a long way from realisation. The enlightenment offered by such study is extremely broad in scope but may be expected to include discoveries about the nature of language and its functioning, many grammars rather than one, language acquisition and development. One example will need to serve as illustrative of the range of possibilities – attitudes to language. Those of us brought up on formal school grammar were led to believe in a single standard: a 'correct' English, governed by laws. This prescriptive (and proscriptive – 'thou shalt not . . .') approach took no account of the constant movement for change in language – slow in syntax, rapid in vocabulary – nor of the conventional origin of many so-called rules. Forbidding the use of a preposition to end a sentence had no *linguistic* justification. Contrast this with the constraints on word order: English allows 'three blind mice' but not 'blind three mice' (unless 'blind' is an imperative verb).

No single book could possibly encompass fully all these areas of practical interest, but Fraser and O'Donnell's *Applied Linguistics and the Teaching of English* with Halliday, McIntosh and Stevens's *The Linguistic Sciences and Language Teaching*, Quirk's *The Use of English* and Doughty, Pearce and Thornton's *Exploring Language* would offer ideas in plenty. A complementary modern study of the art and craft of writing is not so easily found; in the absence of any new work taking as comprehensive a view, *Fundamentals of Good Writing* by Cleanth Brooks and Robert Penn Warren is still a valuable source.

(2) Language study should be set firmly in the linguistic environment of the pupils. Since this is a reiteration, in a different context, of an earlier theme, no extensive elaboration is necessary. Children's intuitive understanding of the workings and possibilities of language needs to be brought to the level of conscious awareness by encouraging them to notice and wonder about all the language transactions they are engaged in. Among the themes that are worth early exploration are variations in formality to suit different purposes and audiences, differences among individuals, leading on to accent and dialect, the language of situations (where a start might be made with games, humour, children's pastimes, 'secret' languages), the contrasts and similarities between speaking and writing.

(3) Language study should be directed at attaining the aim of developing mastery by attention to two means: extending the variety of language experience and encouraging experiment with language. In the first of these, literature has a key part to play, but this has

to be deliberately fostered. Some incidental learning may accrue simply from extensive interaction with what is read and heard, but as a method it is too haphazard to be relied on. A delicate balance needs to be maintained between enjoyment (which should always be paramount) and profit from exploring the ways in which writers achieve their purposes with language. At first this may be no more than the teacher savouring publicly the vividness of a description, the aptness of a metaphor, the creation of suspense, the authenticity of dialogue, and inviting children to be alert for these in their own reading (material for the personal anthologies suggested in Chapter 5). Thereafter, each of these might be further explored and related more and more directly to the children's own writing.

Experiment with language starts from curiosity and wonder, attitudes all too easily stifled in the world of standard exercises. If we invite children to complete dead similes or to fill in sentence blanks from a fixed list of words, we should expect the growth of a belief in a single 'right' solution to all language problems. The true power and flexibility of language resides in the opposite direction; a rich variety of possible answers to each situation, though some will be more effective than others. Some of the range of syntactic possibilities was illustrated in Chapter 4. At word level, one starting point could be a study of synonyms and gradations of meaning among sets. What distinguishes 'bottle' from 'jar'? What is the relationship among 'hatred', 'anger', 'rage', 'fury'? Familiarity with, and confidence in using, a variety of dictionaries and a thesaurus is a vital component of this kind of exploration. The impulse to discover should come specifically from each child's struggle with language. The teacher's task is to point the way not solely to a solution for that problem, but towards the more general language manifestations of which it is just one example.

The analysis in Chapter 4 demonstrates that children do progress in their use of language structures and this happens largely without direct teaching. They follow a common path, though at different speeds and with some variations in what is gathered along the way. Is it enough to offer a wide variety of language experiences and an encouragement to experiment, or is some form of direct intervention worthwhile? Hugh Fraser, in a series called *Control and Create* (intended for backward children in secondary schools, but often adapted for use with juniors), argues the case for deliberate teaching. His 'gradual writing' scheme is based on a grammatical ordering of structures. Children start with simple structures, master them and then move on to more complex forms. In the United States,

John Mellon experimented with sentence-building exercises for secondary pupils, concentrating on the process of embedding: the insertion of additional elements into a basic sentence. Both claim success for their methods: Fraser pointing to improved quality and quantity of writing, Mellon to clear increases in the syntactic versatility of his students. Both, it should be noted, are teaching the use of language, not providing instruction in grammar.

The value of these methods is still open to argument. Children seem to need to go through all the stages described earlier of exploring the resources of language and these stages, as was affirmed then, do not necessarily follow the logic of grammar from simple to more complex. Introducing exercises of these kinds would call for very careful judgement on the teacher's part to make sure the time was right for a new set of constructions. In addition, the sequence of exercises runs counter to an earlier suggestion that exploration of language resources should be firmly set in each child's language experience and problems. More in keeping with this proposition is to find natural starting points. One example is an expansion game played in small groups, where one child supplies a brief starting sentence and others add to it in turn to see how long a sentence can be made. The end result, with older juniors, can then be examined for how well it works. Does it make sense? Is it easy to understand? Can it be abbreviated without losing something essential? Opportunities can be found for exploring some of the devices language offers for carrying out these operations, starting with the ubiquitous 'and', with features like embedding appearing as the children's repertoire increases.

If note-making is encouraged as a regular activity in learning, an even more powerful source of syntactic discovery is made available. Notes are elliptical, contracted, leaving out joinings and expansions. The act of re-creating them in connected prose can also be made the subject of examination and discussion, as an individual or group concern. Exploring the different ways in which a single set of notes can be re-expressed leads to discoveries about the relationship between structure and meaning in a way which sharply enhances awareness of the possibilities in language.

Spelling and Punctuation

Strictly speaking, these terrible twins are part of the preceding section, but deserve separate treatment if for no other reason than that they attract the most, and noisiest, attention. They have tended to be yoked together and used as infallible touchstones of the state of literacy in the young, with each generation bemoaning the current decline from its own high standards and apportioning the blame impartially among teachers, popular culture, the media, the decline of reading, progressive educational dogma and many more.

The first essential in confronting these skills and their acquisition is to separate them and recognise their characteristics. Spelling is a relatively inflexible convention, in which change has been frozen for two centuries and individual freedom of expression confined to trivial instances: judgment or judgement, -ise or -ize, inquire or enquire, phantasy or fantasy. The universal reign of print forbids the anarchy of free-choice spelling; the dictionary has to rule. Punctuation, too, is a convention, but with many fewer restraints on its operation. It translates two sets of signals: one from grammatical structure (like the pair of commas announcing the non-restrictive relative clause), one from the intonation system (where the exclamation mark and question mark indicate different ways of sounding a stretch of language). Each of us is free, within fairly wide limits, to express our individuality in our punctuation as in our handwriting. The punctuation in this book is, or should be, consistent, but it will also be unique in a number of respects. Worth noting, too, is the fact that punctuation habits change quite rapidly, while spelling stands still. The colon and semi-colon have been falling out of fashion, while the dash has become commoner.

English spelling has been a target for ardent reformers and humorists for a very long time. George Bernard Shaw's suggestion that 'ghoti' should be pronounced 'fish' (*gh* as in cough, *o* as in women, *ti* as in notion) has had wide currency. Schemes for simplifying or reforming our system have rested on the claim that spelling in English obeys no rules, has no easily discernible pattern, is in most respects illogical. The absence of perfect regularity is undeniable. Spelling would not need a moment's thought if there were a one to one correspondence between phonemes (the minimum speech sounds) and graphemes (the letters of an alphabet). English possesses 44 phonemes, but only 26 graphemes, some of which are not unique in their representation of sounds: c, s; c, k. Nevertheless, the degree of regularity is surprisingly high: one study by the Americans Paul and Jean Hanna reported a figure of 90 per cent predictability when position in syllables, syllable stress and constraints on orthography are taken into account.

The difficulties are not all in the mind, but they are undoubtedly exaggerated. Both teacher and child are pushed by such propaganda into one of two extreme positions; either to ignore spelling altogether, in the hope that it will be incidentally learnt or at least not create an impenetrable barrier to comprehension, or to become neurotic on one side and anxiously pedantic on the other. A starting attitude of confidence and interest in teacher and learner must be where we begin, but the role of the teacher is paramount. As Margaret Peters has it: 'There is no question that the behaviour of the teacher determines, more than any other single factor, whether a child learns or does not learn to spell' (in *Spelling: Task and Learner* edited by Wade and Wedell).

From this beginning in motivation and attitude, suggestions for action grow naturally. Some arise from themes already discussed; curiosity about language, attention to letter shapes and sequences in reading and more directly in handwriting. Teachers need to know more about the spelling system than dimly-remembered rules. A large group of teachers on an in-service course, asked to quote one such rule, all came up with 'i before e except after c'. None realised that this was only half the rule, omitting the vital 'when the sound is "ee"'. Rules are in any case unhelpful; it is the underlying pattern of systems that matter. Here recent research, such as that described by Ken Albrow in *The English Writing System*, provides not only the information, but material capable of being exploited in teaching.

Children do not need much encouraging to play with words, nor to wonder at the patterns and irregularities they come across. One of our 9-year-old writers was fascinated by the word 'photograph'. 'Why doesn't it begin with f?' After a few more words beginning in the same way (philately, Pharaoh) had emerged from the discussion that followed, someone else noticed that it ended in the same way too. A dictionary search eventually led to the discovery that the ph- was borrowed unchanged from the original Greek words. Then the search was on to explain 'cough' and 'rough'. With the last word a new line of enquiry opens up, the richness of English in homophones (rough, ruff) and the beginnings of a realisation that hidden beneath the surface of spelling are borrowed spelling systems, working in different ways.

A summary of all the potentially relevant implications for teaching arising from enquiries into spelling difficulties would be a very lengthy process, but some key features are worth listing to assist the construction of a policy for spelling.

(1) Whatever the scheme adopted, a teacher must be consistent and rational in its application and in her attitudes towards the skill.
(2) The use of published spelling lists as a basis for work is much less effective than material gathered from her children's own needs and difficulties.
(3) Rote correction of errors (rewriting correctly) is much less efficient

than guiding children towards an understanding of their characteristic errors.
(4) There is no time when attention to the shaping of words is inappropriate, though it needs to be separated from writing for younger
junior pupils while confidence and fluency are established.
(5) Autonomy in using a dictionary should be a high priority, together
with encouragement for children to 'sound out' words and to experiment with spelling before seeking assistance.
(6) Since spelling confusions can be both visual and vocal-auditory in
origin, discrimination in both modes should be systematically developed, most effectively by the link with reading. Note though
that the sound of words precedes visual experience by a very long
way in children's encounters with language. In the early stages of
work with the shape of words, visual experience needs to pre-
dominate in order to redress the balance.

Many teachers will have had the experience of attempting to teach
some feature of punctuation, either as part of a regular programme or
as a response to an apparent need in their pupils. Exercises designed to
consolidate understanding are tackled with commendable accuracy, but
subsequent written work is a disappointment. In one case, all trace of
what has been taught has utterly vanished, in another the chosen feature
is everywhere and anywhere. A plausible explanation for this is that
the purpose of punctuation does not get due attention: these extra
marks on the page are understood to be just optional decorations. If
children are at an early stage introduced to the idea that punctuation
marks, like letter shapes, help translate speech into writing, this mis-
understanding is much less likely to arise.

A decision on what marks to acknowledge necessarily precedes consideration of how to treat them. The full-stop is of vital importance,
with its tone variants the question mark and exclamation mark. The
delight of younger juniors in creating dialogue (noted earlier) suggests
that inverted commas should be included. The comma, for which more
than forty separate functions are listed in some textbooks, is a much less
certain choice. Two uses merit selection for their frequency and consistency in writing. The first finds the comma signalling the omission of
a word. 'That old, black, limping, bright-eyed dog' has commas standing
in for the conjunction 'and'. As it works in joining single words, so it
does with phrases and clauses. 'He walked in, looked round, blinked in
the bright light and sat down.' The second employs the comma as a
separating device, marking off additions or modifications to a main

statement. 'John, bring your book here.' 'After lighting the fire, she made the tea.' 'Edward the Seventh, King of England, died in 1910.'

Helping children to understand and employ this minimum set of marks belongs to the second stage of writing, after the physical skills are firmly established. On method there is much less certainty; it is perhaps significant that the Bullock Report offers an annex on spelling to its chapter on writing, but says nothing of punctuation. Teachers have experimented with some success on listening for intonation cues as a technique – the characteristic fall-rise of the question, the rise-fall of exclamation, the fall denoting sentence end. The close connection with reading skills is a strong recommendation for a trial of this method, though it probably needs reinforcing with more direct work on identifying sentence and non-sentence. A careful and slow reading on tape, with natural pauses slightly lengthened, is an aid to identifying comma placings, with children working on an unpunctuated version of the text being read. Only a small minority of children are likely, at the end of their fourth junior year, to have attained sufficient skill in reading aloud to use this as a self-correction method with their own work, but it is worth trying. Fostering an increasing interest in the way reading material is punctuated should not be overlooked – the exuberance of Roald Dahl's exclamation marks, the extensive use of colon and semi-colon in Lewis Carroll contrasted with the dashes and staccato sentences of Ted Hughes.

Preparation

Most discussions of the teaching of writing in schools somewhere include the assertion that talk must come first. A representative expression of this belief is John Dixon's : 'writing assignments without a background of discussion and shared experience are unlikely to elicit much response from many children and young people' (from Chapter 3 of *Growth through English*). Talk is a most satisfying and immediate way of responding to experience, and sharing with others helps us to extend and modify our understanding. There are some who suspect this easy conclusion on the value of language, a doubt memorably expressed by Robert Graves in his poem 'The Cool Web', where words are condemned for filtering out much of the direct impact of events. Nevertheless, the general principle seems to be a sound one; beginning writers are likely to be aided by the opportunity to rehearse in speech their own ideas and to overhear the thoughts of others.

To build this into our practice as a universal principle would, however, be a mistake. Considerations of purpose and audience need to be taken into account. No public preliminaries are necessary for much of the expressive writing which falls under Moffett's heading of 'reflection': diary, autobiography, note-making. Different *kinds* of talk are required by different functions. If the intended writing is transactional, discussion will aim at convergence on a series of solutions; it will provide answers, guide selection, support memory, while not necessarily excluding speculation nor individual interpretation. There will be an agreed common core to the writing that follows to fit the demands of the experience. Where the movement is towards the poetic, discussion travels outwards into the exploratory, the tentative. The focus shifts from explanation to speculation; there can be no agreed solutions. The question that expresses this stance most directly is 'I wonder what would happen if . . . ?'

The practice of beginning a writing programme with extensive experience of group and class oral composition has been widely employed, often with impressive results. Not only is there a confidence boost for the least articulate in being able to make a contribution relatively painlessly, but the process of shaping a narrative is being explored out in the open. The potential danger in the method is that, carried on for too long, it may obstruct the development of individual imagining in much the same way as strongly teacher-directed discussion does. A more insidious danger results from over-conscientiousness in pursuing preliminary talk. An exciting theme can be talked to death long before the first word arrives on paper, after its every nuance has been relentlessly run down and triumphantly listed on the board.

Our own enquiry added a significant dimension to a study of the effects of preparation. For factual writing, few differences emerged in the language resources employed, whether there had been full verbal preparation, or none. The figures for creative writing produced a surprising result. Though the pieces preceded by normal preparation were slightly longer than those undertaken without discussion, they were less mature, judged by the language measures we were examining. Table 13 shows the size of these differences on the six variables selected earlier: sentence length, clause length, subordination index, Loban index, uncommon clauses and personal pronoun index. Only variable 5 (uncommon clauses) shows no advantage for the unprepared writing.

Table 13 *Differences between prepared and unprepared creative writing*

Variable	1	2	3	4	5	6
Prepared	9·0	6·5	17·0	3·1	25·0	12·6
Unprepared	9·6	6·9	19·0	3·5	25·0	12·2

The prepared pieces may be of better quality, though a comparative reading suggests, on the basis of subjective impressions, that this is not generally true. The evidence of a narrowing of language experiment is firm enough to indicate that full verbal preparation for writing should not be an habitual practice. We may, in over-employing this approach, set boundaries for the writer of which we are unaware and inadvertently hinder the development in written language we are trying so hard to promote. In addition, the self-motivating writer is less likely to emerge, if these are the standard conditions for work.

Two final themes deserve attention as part of preparation, though they are strictly concerned with the act of writing rather than what goes before it. The first of these has given rise to one of those arguments which are likely to appear when any two or more teachers talk about methods of teaching English skills. Should writing be a workshop activity or not? The workshop approach places the writer in a professional context, appraising material, function, audience, working through a series of approximations until a final, satisfying draft emerges. One expression of this view was referred to in the last chapter, where Peter Doughty argued for reworking of writing as a necessary aid in transferring from hesitant command to fluent command. Indeed, he calls the four-stage process of development, from recognition to fluent command, 'rehearsal'.

The counter-proposition is forcefully expressed by James Britton. 'We shape language most effectively *at the point of utterance*. Planning ahead, in any detailed form, tends to be more of a hindrance than a help . . . we are able to talk or write our way into a situation – and out again at the far end' (introduction to *Talking and Writing*). These two positions are not, at root, incompatible. Every act of writing is likely to involve some rehearsal, in the head. Grierson (in *Rhetoric and English Composition*) quotes the great eighteenth-century historian Edward Gibbon on the process. 'It has always been my practice to cast a long paragraph in a single mould, to try it by my ear, to deposit it in my memory, but to suspend the action of the pen till I had given the last polish to my work.'

The practical solution seems to be to make some use of both approaches, taking due account not only of material, audience and purpose, but also the age and skill of the writers. Junior-school children rarely correct or revise of their own volition, except to change obvious errors, and hardly ever express dissatisfaction with a piece of writing, once complete. The reason is plain enough: the ability to detach oneself from one's own efforts, to view them objectively and to assess their fitness for an intended purpose, is learnt over considerable periods of time and often with great difficulty. A start, though, on this learning is possible relatively early in the junior school. Most children by this time are experts in responding to narrative fiction and are beginning to develop a critical apparatus for expressing those responses. They may find it hard to explain why they like a particular story, but cope more confidently with dislikes. With alert and interested pupils as audience, a child writer, working in narrative fiction where his strength and confidence are greatest, will be fed with general and particular criticism.

Naturally enough, the rules of these encounters need careful framing and children chosen to present their work for their capacity to profit from the exchange. By the end of the third year and through the fourth, our evidence pointed to a period of consolidation, when pupils begin to reduce or stabilise output of writing and to slow their advance towards linguistic maturity. With some experience of the audience participation just described, this appears to be the time to encourage such children to start the next step, not only responding to an audience, but anticipating its response. Even at this stage, for most children the most advantageous method seems to be 'rehearsal in the head' rather than the painstaking and time-consuming redrafting technique of the mature writer. This has solid justification at later stages of writing development, but delays the satisfaction of producing completed work too long for the young writer.

The last consideration relates to the setting in which the writing takes place. Not so long ago, the possible variations would have been few; writing tended to be overwhelmingly a class lesson. More recently the change to group and individual working, the end of timetable rigidity, the use of vertical grouping have made this less likely. Certainly much of the expressive-transactional writing arising in project and topic work is necessarily undertaken when the need arises. 'Free' and 'intensive' writing, and some forms of creative writing derived from them demand a collective writing act, immediately following the shared stimulus. Other kinds, notably those that have been described as a kind of expressive autobiography, need no formal setting within the range of learning activities.

Yet the question arises, whether some circumstances are more propitious than others in aiding the beginning writer. M. Hourd and G. Cooper, commenting on their poetry writing experiments with third and fourth year juniors in *Coming into Their Own* were in no doubt. They maintain that the act of writing in a group heightened attention and intensified co-operation. Marie Peel, in *Seeing to the Heart*, speaks of the need to create the right atmosphere for writing: engendering slight tension, anticipation and a marked reduction in noise levels. Our observations of the project children at work suggested that in this, as in so much else, they exhibited a variety of preferences. Some were easily distracted by other activities going on around them and their writing progressed in fits and starts, if at all. Others seemed able to shut themselves off completely, though these were few. Most seemed to gain from an awareness of a common activity surrounding them; the re-assurance perhaps of seeing and feeling others engaged on a related task.

If these observations are more than just random impressions, they point to the need for a conscious concern with the physical conditions for writing. Younger and less confident pupils in particular will require the most advantageous settings we can devise; freedom from distractions, low noise levels, a sense of community from others engaged on the same activity. In semi-open-plan and open-plan schools, the creation of quiet writing areas should have as high a priority as quiet reading areas, though this is not to advocate the return of the silent classroom. Children need to interact in these early steps towards writing mastery, but on their initiative; this is not distraction but support. Concentration comes under attack from the variety of activities and experiences unrelated to writing that constantly flow in and around the school. One vivid picture sums this up; one of our project group engaged on a poem retreating first to a corridor, then to the hall and finally to a cloakroom, using the coats as a baffle for sound, only to give up when the recorder group also took refuge there.

THE TREATMENT OF WRITING

When we undertake the long and unendingly complex task of learning to use language, a relatively early discovery is that the only feedback available is a response from other human beings (or its absence). Children do rehearse new possibilities on their own (see, for instance, the pre-sleep monologues examined by Ruth Weir in *Language in the Crib*), but they must test their discoveries on other language users. If learning is to be efficient and uninterrupted, these responses need to be readily and regularly available, as the retardation in language development of children in institutions amply confirms.

Though the act of writing may separate writer from reader in both time and space, unlike most speech situations, the need for a response remains unaltered, even if, in some reflective forms of writing, it is the writer's other self that reacts. To amend an assertion discarded earlier, we learn to write by writing and *noting its effects*. In determining what part we as teachers should play in these transactions, our attention falls inevitably on the three fundamental components: the writer, his purpose, his audience. We need a repertoire of responses which we then try to match exactly to each occasion. Too often, because of pressure of time or uncertainty about what would be appropriate, the temptation is to fall back on a stock answer: a tick, a star, a 'good work', 'I'll put that on display'. As James Moffett puts it: 'A response must be real and pertinent to the action, not a standard "professional" reaction. Any unvarying response, positive or not, teaches us nothing about the effects of what we have done.'

Where the purpose is plain and the audience some outside agency, as in the case of letter-writing or providing information, feedback is usually direct and needs only to be explored for the lessons it offers. The bulk of junior-school writing is, however, directed at internal audiences: the writer himself, his fellow-pupils, the teacher.

If, as was advocated earlier, we should make the maximum use of other children as a real and responsive audience, they clearly need help in understanding and interpreting this role. The teacher for this purpose acts as a model, so that the rules of the critical game are gradually assimilated. At least as important as the rules is the demonstration of attitude; enthusiasm and respect for what is offered will indicate the seriousness and importance of the activity. The effect is likely to be beneficial on writer as well as audience in that if a teacher shows her conviction that writing is important, children will be readier to produce it. Conversely, children will adapt to a superficial assessment of their work by writing superficially. There is ample evidence that they very quickly learn to give the school what it appears to want, in this activity as in all the others.

Ways of sharing writing efforts satisfyingly pose a constant challenge to the teacher. Reading aloud, by writer, classmate or teacher, is the most direct method and has a claim to being the most frequently used. Exchanges among pupils appear to be very much less common, though, with the appropriate guidance in constructive response, the economy of effort is clearly worthwhile. Enlarging the circle of readers beyond the single class, especially where a common interest offers a strong inducement, has its merits too. In one of the project schools a second- and a fourth-year class were working independently and at different levels on the topic 'Time'. They were encouraged to talk to each other about the discoveries, to look at the writing, artwork and models that had emerged and finally created a joint display. To the outside observer, both parties appeared to have benefited considerably from the experience.

More indirect is the practice of displaying work, mounted in books or on wall spaces. Teachers differ very markedly in their views on this.

Of the fifty teachers who worked on the project, five, for a variety of reasons, rejected the practice. Most were moderate users, while three maintained that it should have the highest priority and expended great efforts in support of their beliefs. No one who, as a visitor to a class-room and reading the material on display, has been besieged by authors eager to identify and talk about their work, can doubt the value of the recognition offered by the act of publication. What is sometimes lacking is evidence that attention is strongly directed to encouraging reading and reaction to what is displayed. The wall-mounted work quickly becomes invisible, the handsomely-produced books dusty relics without such attention.

The controversy on whether only 'fair' copies should be displayed, or the originals, warts and all, still engenders some heat. A number of teachers get round the difficulty by typing those pieces destined for public view, adding a little deft editing as they do so. The argument for corrected versions is sound, as far as it goes, but the penalties may seem unacceptably heavy. Few children enjoy copying for its own sake, and this teacher's experience has been that for every 'error' removed, a new one is likely to appear unbidden. The chance of diminishing enthusiasm for writing is very real. If children are alert to spot mistakes and their fellow-pupils encouraged to help, the important revisions (inserting missing words, increasing legibility) can be carried out without difficulty on the original in readiness for display. Worth remembering too is the effect on those children still in the early stages of struggling with the skill. They certainly need the sense of pride in achievement offered by a display of their work, but are much less likely to be selected if the criterion of choice is ability to produce an impressively neat and error-free copy.

Thus far, reference to judgement of quality has been, at most, indirect. Readers will remember that the original enquiry made no attempt to explore this dimension of response to writing, though it was argued in Chapter 4 that the range of language resources deployed and skill in their use would make important contributions to such judgements. Assessment in this broad sense is an inescapable part of our response to any experience and must have a high priority for teachers whose aim is to help children advance in their mastery of a complex and subtle craft.

Misunderstandings have arisen over this function of assessment most often because its nature has been misinterpreted. It is not just error-hunting, nor deliberating between 'good' and 'very good' as a concluding comment, nor ensuring that a mark book has its proper quota of entries. Assessment is a considered response to a piece of writing, taking account of its purpose, its intended audience, the situation of the writer and his writing history, leading to suggestions for more effective realisations of the thoughts, feelings, information, arguments that the writer is trying to express.

If this definition is accepted as a just description of the teacher's concern, its corollary is the central requirement that, for success, the teacher must be a skilled and sensitive reader, as David Holbrook has for so long argued and convincingly demonstrated (e.g. in *English for the Rejected*). As part of in-service courses on children's writing, I have often asked primary teachers to read a piece stripped of all identifying elements and to search for answers to a set of questions. What is there to be learnt about the writer from the writing? What circumstances were created by the teacher as a preliminary to writing? How would you respond to the writing? What growth points are there for development? What difficulties does the writer have and how might he be helped to tackle them?

Many of those audiences were doubtful whether anything useful could be deduced with so little information, but they all good-naturedly agreed to try. Invariably the result was one of considerable surprise, that their intuitions chimed with the factual information, and that the level of agreement among themselves on qualitative aspects was so high. Readers might like to try themselves on one of the pieces used in this way and compare their findings with the summary contained in parentheses following the writing.

Eternal Heart-break

'John looked up the mountain. The rain poured steadily down, it tapped on the window with its' icy fingers. John was alone, His mother was dead and his father was somewhere in those towering grey mountains. John's father had been gone two days and John was lonely. Food had run out the nearest store was ten miles away. The boy was heart-broken. In his anxiety for his dearly beloved father John had not slept but stayed by that window tired and hungry. Then John saw someone coming down the side of the mountain. His face brightened for a brief moment. But then he saw it was only the guide with his dog, a black and white collie. John's face fell. It was an endless wait and eternal heartbreak. Suddenly John realised the aweful truth. His father was dead. He must be. No one had told him anything. He was lying dead on the mountain-side. Thoughts of this disasterous scene whirled through his head. He uttered a loud scream and fell onto the bed. There he lay for days awaiting the return of a man who would never come.'

(The writer is Wendy, the second-year junior whose account of her class outing to Stapleford Park was reproduced in Chapter 2. The strong visual emphasis suggests a visual stimulus – in fact a picture of high, bleak mountains. The very 'literary' style and the flavour of some of the clichés – eternal heartbreak, dearly beloved father, uttered a loud scream – suggests an avid reader drawing freely on her memory. The consistency of tone points to minimum verbal preparation, rather than full class discussion. With her command of technical features in writing and her confidence, most readers suggested that Wendy was ready for critical suggestions in order to encourage the development of self-appraisal. One possibility recurred as a starting point for guiding her towards examining the credibility of the narrative – why didn't John go out to the guide and ask for help?)

From alert and responsive reading the next step is an attempt to crystallise what one is looking for. General criteria for judgement and appreciation need to be listed, examined and their relevance for our apprentice writers carefully weighed. Among those that would appear high in order of importance on most lists would be such considerations as: order, coherence, appropriateness of emphasis and of form, ease of understanding, completeness, absence of ambiguity (while acknowledging the special case of literature), effectiveness for purpose, interest, inventiveness, euphony. Holbrook, in his discussion of the reader's task in *Children's Writing*, includes sincerity and realism, with the former recognised by the freshness, energy, rhythm, feeling for language displayed in the writing (the identification of this quality is not easy, though – is Wendy's writing sincere, or not?)

All of these, to a greater or lesser extent depending on the writing's purpose, play a part in determining how we feel about the experience offered. It would be absurd, of course, to apply this formidable battery of tests, together with considerations of punctuation and spelling, level of language performance, indiscriminately to every piece we are presented with. Simplistic solutions are no real answer either; those for instance which advocate leaving creative writing alone and heaping the burden of assessment on to factual material.

Discussions of this topic, particularly in relation to the work of younger children, seem in the end to come down to a series of general guides to action:

(1) establish quantity before quality; children who are anticipating an assault on their work are likely to attend only to the mechanical aspects of the skill and will lose all chance of fluency and confidence;

(2) reinforce what is good, look for and praise points of growth and development before attending to difficulties;

(3) try to make time to talk to each child about his writing, but ensure that positive comments are written on the piece, too; the effects last longer and are immediately accessible;

(4) arrange an order of importance among the merits to be encouraged; in the early stages order, coherence and clarity are of much greater significance than how the writing reads, or sounds;

(5) challenge children to become effective critics of their own work in as many ways as possible, helping them to develop a responsiveness to the demands of purpose and audience;

(6) avoid the temptation of making direct suggestions for alterations and revisions, so that the work remains a consistent whole; letting writers know what we feel, what we are reminded of, asking questions, are potent and valuable indirect influences on subsequent writing.

8

The Difficulties of Writing

'The dull child will go ahead only when he thinks he knows exactly where he stands and exactly what is ahead of him. If he does not feel he knows exactly what an experience will be like, and if it will not be exactly like other experiences he already knows, he wants no part of it.'
(John Holt – *How Children Fail*)

'Why did I write? What sin to me unknown
Dipped me in ink, my parents', or my own?
As yet a child, nor yet a fool to fame,
I lisped in numbers, for the numbers came.'
(Alexander Pope – *Epistle to Dr Arbuthnot*)

Robert, at the time of the first major collection of writing during the enquiry, was a member of a first-year junior class of thirty-six. At 7 years 8 months he represented the average age of the group. Well-adjusted on the evidence of his score on the Bristol Social Adjustment Guide (a single negative point), he also scored slightly above average on both the verbal and non-verbal tests. He was the younger in a family of two children, his father a skilled worker and both parents respected by his teachers for the keen but not excessive interest they took in his progress at school. When we observed him in school surroundings, he came over as an energetic, confident boy, interested in most of his work, able to concentrate successfully for good periods of time and fluent in speech, though occasionally getting into a tangle in explaining his ideas fully.

At first sight these details seem to indicate the profile of an average or slightly above average pupil, whose writing one would predict to be at an equivalent stage to that of Mark, the first-year representative in the Chapter 4 examples. The reality is rather different. For the first collection he wrote four pieces: the first based on a picture story of two parrots and a small girl, the second resulting from a discussion of two tracks of a long-playing record where music was used to suggest witches and then strange animals, the third a response to a television programme on bears and the last following talk about the children's weekend experiences.

(1) 'Nan and Nim had a nott from Jane and Nan had a pak and than they had bof a pak and they bof had fit and Jan was cries and Jane mummy cam and they stoped and Nan a apple and Nim was cries.'
(2) 'the witchs are in the cave makeing the spels mabe of a spiddes lag and a bit of spid and witches spells.'
(3) 'Bears live in iceland and they are poler bears and they eat fish and Brown Bears eat honey and when they have BaBey the mummy taks them out and they play.'
(4) 'on Friday me and And rew went swiming and we swum 2 wivs.'

His class teacher confirmed that these closely resembled in fluency, content and control his general response to the task of writing. Sixteen months later, when Robert was nine, the last of our collections was produced. On this occasion the four writing situations were:

(a) after children had been caught in a heavy rainstorm the day before, a record of storm sound effects was played;
(b) Bubble-blowing – children encouraged to catch and describe a bubble – its colours, reflections particularly – with reinforcement from a poem about a boy blowing bubbles who imagines himself inside one;
(c) after undertaking seed-sowing, following work-card instructions, children asked to describe what they had done;
(d) 'Polly the Clock' – a play performed in school by the Playhouse schools company, with a good deal of audience participation. Children talked about the experience and what they had enjoyed in it, before writing.

(1) 'On day I was at the swimming baths and there was a storm and when we got out of the swimming baths there was a storm so we whent under a tree for shelter but the storm was getting worser so we ran the rest of the way home and when we gor home we where socked so our mothers gor us a cup of tea and the we went to bed whith a cold.'
(2) 'One day I was blowing bubbles. In my garden and I bluw a bubble and it gruw and gruw til it landed and I steped in the bubble and everything was made of bubble even the people the people had one little bubble for there hed and two little bubbles for there arms and

to qieut little bubble for there legs all of a sudden I started to get hungery so I felt in my pocket and I felt a bit of metel and I droped it and the buble poped and it was all a dream.'

(3) 'First we got a plant pot and fild it up with soil and put our name tag in it and then we put the seeds in the cane and then we put soil cane and we tied it to giver and we put the cane in the plant pot.'

(Note: 'cane' is a short length of hollow bamboo cane.)

(4) 'Once upon a time there was a village and in the village there was a clock called poly and in the clock called poly there was all the villages treasure and at night Tikup looked after the clock so nobody stole the treasure and that the clock wouldnt stop but one night ticup set a trap in case anybody tried to steel the treasure.'

No elaborate analysis is necessary to show the advance in fluency, control and confidence achieved by Robert from the first to the second set. Measures of syntactic progress confirm the overall impression that, though Robert was struggling to make sense of the mysteries of writing at first, he is now much clearer in his understanding of the business, though still a very long way from mastery, and not yet within reach of the performance his ability and circumstances seem to promise. His is not an uncommon case, but this does not make a satisfying explanation any easier to produce. Something held him back initially and this slow start carries the threat that he might always be lagging behind his peers, with undesirable effects on his interest and confidence. Whether that something was illness, early reading problems, deficiencies in his infant school learning, motivation or an entirely different cause, there is no way of being certain. His advance from these hesitant beginnings probably owes much to his good fortune in being with the same teacher for two years and to her meticulously careful and sensitive work with him. Robert is clearly not one of the type of less-able children that Holt describes in the quotation at the head of this chapter; equally he is not the effortlessly natural writer of Pope's self-portrait (Wendy seems to fit comfortably into that frame).

The case of Ian, Robert's classmate, is significantly different and a more formidable challenge to teaching skill. Just three weeks younger, he was the middle child in a family of three, while his father's occupation placed him in the Registrar-General's class V (unskilled). A social adjustment score of 30 set him clearly in the maladjusted group, though he was not immediately the child an outside observer would have noticed for his behaviour. Not an inveterate talker, over the two years of the enquiry he became more easily distracted, harder to interest in anything for any length of time. His score in the verbal test was close to the average for the whole sample of children, though his non-verbal performance was well down.

His efforts on the two sets of writing situations follow. It should be noted that only the last two pieces in the second set were entirely un-aided; his teacher talked to him, prompted him and, for the first piece, wrote at his dictation. Ian missed the stimulus for the second piece and chose to write instead in response to some poems about snow.

(1) 'Jane gives Nam and Nim an apple. They fight. Jane cries. Jane's mummy comes. She tells them off.'
(2) 'Snow is wit snow is soft snow ig cod i dont like snow much becuas the cars get stuck.'
(3) 'I like beirs I like bears. Bears like honey Bears like to play.'
(4) 'I saw on television a Rommchariot and they had a batt bettent Queen of Shebba.'

(second set)

(1) 'I was playing out in the sun and a storm came.'
(2) 'I was blow bubbles I blow a big bubble it did not pop I got inside it I sor bubbles the haws was bubbles the trees was bubbles the bird was bubbles.'
(3) 'We put the pias in the babaw stik then Simn tod the cottn wiyd I hodd the stik then we put the stik into the codbad pot and tow con owle wat theom was awek and som or groing.'
(We put the pansies in the bamboo stick, then Simon tied the cotton while I held the stick. Then we put the stick into the card-board pot and you can only water them once a week and some are growing.)
(4) 'In a tawn thear livd a clok and is nam was pole the clok and the owne was ticup and he lookt aft the clok and it got cowd and a man cowd Black Jack and he wand the goled and tickop and black jac had a tog war and ticop won the gold and Tikcop was made [the chief clock winder].'

Ian is not standing still, as these last two pieces testify, but his for-ward momentum is very slight and the context for writing is clearly of critical importance; pieces 1 and 4 in the second set were written just a week apart. With all the information immediately present in his memory and to some extent still physically in front of him, he creates a methodical description of events he took part in and a narrative, maintaining chronology successfully. Set to make his own way without these aids, as in the first situation, he sees no way past his brief opening statement. In written language development terms he is still at the 6-year-old level and only falteringly there. If favourable circumstances and good teaching achieve only this much in two years, is Ian's a lost cause?

The difficulties of writing haunt all of us on at least some of the occasions when we wait for inspiration, pen in hand, staring at a blank sheet of paper. At the exalted level of the poet, Yeats's struggle to find something to write about has already been quoted in Chapter 5; T. S. Eliot talks of the 'intolerable wrestle' with words, when language seems unable to take the strain of communicating his meaning exactly. A letter of condolence, communications involving persuasion or exculpation initiate those difficult questions – what shall I say? how shall I say it? These situations differ from Ian's in degree, not in kind. What the mature adult possesses (and this can often be as much hindrance as help) is a range of experience to be inspected, to see if anything will answer the immediate demand or is capable of adaptation. The adult too can objectify the exchange by putting himself in the place of the recipient and judging effects from there: detecting condescension, insincerity, ambiguity, arrogance.

What makes the treatment of young writers' difficulties so uncertain is the puzzle set by trying to account for them. Looking for a match with Ian in respect of age, position in family, home circumstances, behaviour, test performance produces, by a curious chance, another Ian. His first piece for the project, unaided and in controlled, clear handwriting, is:

'Bears live in the caves. The bears eat sweet things. Their cubs liv in the caves with there mother and sometimes there mother taces them in to the forest for play and then they go back to the caves.'

His final effort, sixteen months later:

'One day I went to the woods with my gang. We bilt a tree house. first we had to gather all the wood. then we had to bild a ladder to go up the tree then we started to bild it. After we bilt it we got some old chairs to put in the tree. Then we put in a big table afterwards. I am robin hood with my meery band of men. We got the kings men to have a figth with them and took lady marren. I will marry her so that she can be my wedid wife. Then she can be one of the robin hood gang and we can kill the king.'

On both occasions he is linguistically in advance of Ian, and of Robert too, confident in meeting writing demands. The inevitable conclusion is that, with only partial information on all the relevant circumstances and conditions relating to any child, no possibility exists for pointing to one element and concluding that the explanation lies there. The discussion in Chapter 4 suggested that some elements were more influential than others, but no more than that. The corollary, with its attendant implications for teaching strategies, is that no two children can possibly be treated as alike. If they appear to have similar problems, the chances are that the causes will be unalike, or at best will overlap to only a limited extent. A single, undifferentiated programme for children with writing difficulties is ruled out.

The range of possible expedients in remedial work is very wide and decisions on choice, order, timing will necessarily be affected by a careful study of each child's case. The first Ian was, not unexpectedly, a slow and hesitant reader, needing reassurance even when he was right. He had had little experience of phonics in his infants' school, but was taken out for remedial reading regularly in the juniors, with phonics as the main method of help. The speaking-reading-writing link provided by the *Breakthrough to Literacy* scheme might have been a useful stimulus for him, establishing some initial fluency in producing language, as well as in decoding it. In speech he was not reluctant, but rarely an initiator; as a listener he showed signs of being only fitfully attentive. Ideally he needed ample opportunities for practising conversations with a sympathetic adult, being prompted into taking a lead and developing his listening span at the same time. In the absence of favourable class size and teaching auxiliaries, a tape recorder can substitute for some of these functions, particularly in encouraging fluency. With the beginnings of a grasp of narrative appearing in his second-year writing, recording stories and descriptions of events would help to secure and extend that understanding.

His behaviour problems seem closely bound up with his learning difficulties, though identifying cause and effect is not simple, as was argued in an earlier chapter. It is reasonably certain that he would benefit from feeling success in an activity undeniably his, such as might be provided by a personal diary: dictating entries to teacher (or older, highly literate child) and moving then from tracing over the entries, to copying and on to supervised solo efforts. The need to consider carefully the provision of a congenial setting for writing, a theme elaborated in Chapter 7, is of extra importance for Ian and his fellow beginners. Here experiment is surely worthwhile to discover the most advantageous conditions; separated from the class or working with it, in a class writing session or as occasion offers, beginning or end of a day and so on. It is likely, too, that work by these children will need immediate and extensive reinforcement if time can be made: finding successes to praise, reading aloud, an immediate decision to display carried out there and then.

Running parallel to these specific efforts in advancing writing skill and confidence should be a concern for enlarging language experience. Poor readers, as most of these children will be, are too concerned with the mechanics of reading to be aware of the language variations they are grappling with; these will in any case be limited by the level of the text. Persuading skilled readers in the class to read to them, providing stories on tape for them to enjoy will present them with an extra set of opportunities to become acquainted with new stretches of language. Some of this will be assimilated, some will activate parts of the learner's language resources and encourage their use, while the more abstract qualities of narrative – order, coherence, emphasis, selection, interest – are becoming more familiar, especially if a response is encouraged to the qualities of these experiences. If some of what he hears in this way is the writing of his fellow pupils, the learner's fear of the abstractness and mystery of the writing process stands some chance of being lessened.

With confidence, interest and a motivation to succeed beginning to grow as combinations of these efforts take effect, the general guidance on writing – from experience, for an audience, with a purpose – becomes more prominent. It is certainly not enough for Ian simply to encourage him to write to a fixed pattern. Equally it would be counterproductive to require him to attempt kinds of writing for which his experience and skill are totally inadequate. Here some consideration of the progressions in writing, outlined in Chapter 6, would help plan the way forward, but at a more considered pace than that appropriate for children of average attainment.

Severe restrictions on syntax and vocabulary are a temptation for the teacher to provide direct assistance. Ian employs only one subordination in all his eight pieces and he is still at the stage when the textual 'and' is his universal conjunction. Though we gathered no evidence directly on the effects of particular kinds of language intervention by the teacher, a subjective assessment of the practices in these and many other classrooms suggests that timing is critical. In the earlier discussion on 'and' as a component in writing development, the point was made that even the most able children still resort to its 'textual' use on some occasions, right to the end of their junior school careers, even though they demonstrate their familiarity with a wide variety of other joining devices. Too early an intervention in Ian's case, pointing him towards other systems, would deprive him of this apparently necessary developmental experience. Similar caution is needed with subordination; Ian is well short of the stage where he can begin to comprehend the subtle distinctions in meaning and style brought about by structural changes. To tell him that 'While it was raining I went on the roundabout and fell off' is in some way preferable to 'It was raining and I went on the roundabout and I fell off' is to give him an inflexible rule whose rationale is beyond him.

There is of course no reason why the sentence expansion and sentence joining games advocated earlier should be avoided by Ian, provided they are separated from his writing. What we hope for him at his stage is that he will store away some of this experience and make it his own for later use.

On the contentious subjects of spelling and punctuation, assertions become more vehement with every move down the ability scale. If it is somehow wrong to draw the attention of average junior-school writers to these perils, it must be doubly foolish to burden the strugglers with them. Without repeating the discussion undertaken in the previous chapter, the reverse is true. Ian needs more help, and earlier. Margaret Peters put the case simply on spelling: 'It is the less-favoured child who vitally needs to be taught what he has not been fortunate enough to have caught.' For him, with his limited and hard-won experience of what language looks like, confidence does not come from covering a page with quasi-writing which he is then challenged to translate, but from a few lines which his reader instantly decodes. The interrelating of writing and reading is essential for Ian, so that the shapes of words build up more rapidly into familiar patterns. The beginnings in dictation and copying will habituate him to the notion of accuracy and will reduce the confusions resulting from his making and seeing faulty spelling.

Ian is representative of the writing beginners and yet unique. Individual pieces of his work closely resemble those of many in his position, but the sequence of change, advance, hesitation, confusion is his alone. The suggestions made for remedial action in his case are capable of application to others, but not as a complete package of measures. Which to try, in what order, for how long, with what kinds of supplementary assistance will be determined by the teacher's assessment of each child's situation. The most valuable skill in this area, as it is for all writing, is bound to be the teacher's ability to go beyond the surface of the words on the page; accurate and sensitive diagnosis of problems and incipient triumphs is the key to effective and timely action. It is perhaps worth repeating a belief that for the teacher to practise the art of writing freely is to enhance this skill, among others.

What might be referred to as the 'higher-order' difficulties of writing – organising information effectively, avoiding obscurity and ambiguity, matching manner and matter, interpreting a writing task accurately, acquiring a sense of the varying demands of purpose and audience – have been the concern of all that has gone before and require no additional commentary. There is no escape from the unremitting challenge that the craft and art of writing offers, except on the most routine of occasions. The most desirable achievement in teaching writing is not necessarily a collection of instant anthology material, but evidence that children have the resources to cope sensibly and effectively with any writing situation, and the confidence to use those resources intelligently.

One last illustration from the project analysis will serve as a cautionary postscript, a way of reiterating that what is known about writing and writers and how they are related amounts at most to the equivalent of one word on a printed page. On three occasions spread through the two years of the enquiry, our 290 children were observed in their usual classroom activities, once in the morning and again in the afternoon. These observing sessions fulfilled a number of purposes, among which was an attempt to discover the characteristic behaviour of each child on three distinct dimensions, for which the labels talkativeness, activity, absorption offer a description. Each dimension incorporated four scale positions as, for example, very talkative, moderately talkative, moderately silent, very silent. Children were rated on these scales by the observer, not directly, but by reference to the range and kind of behaviour noted under different headings.

The numbers of children falling into the four talkative-silent categories emerged as 53 : 95 : 88 : 53 and these groups were then used as a basis for a further consideration of the writing they produced. The groups proved to be comparable in age distribution, balance of the sexes, average test scores and Registrar-General's classification so that contrasts among their performances in writing were possible. Not surprisingly, the more talkative a child, the higher his social adjustment score was likely to be, though the differences among groups were not large. Again according to expectation, the very talkative group showed up as much less fluent in writing than the very silent: a difference in average total output of 2,500 to 3,100 words. The size of the difference was a surprise; the very talkative group included not only the inveterate chatterers, but also the energetic, purposeful, curiosity-driven children. Equally the very silent group was composed of the self-sufficient, absorbed, well organised, together with the reserved, inactive day-dreamers.

The work of the very silent group on analysis proved generally to be slightly more mature in syntactic terms than that of their vocal counter-parts; they performed rather better than their test scores suggested they might. Much more significant was a major contrast in the way the two groups employed personal pronouns. As the details in Chapter 4 indicated, a preference for first-person pronouns gradually asserts itself over the early choice of third person, so that the two are more or less equally favoured by the fourth year. Within this overall pattern, the very talkative group appeared to resist the change; they start with a sharply marked preference for 'he', 'they' and move much more slowly to 'I' and 'we'. Exactly the reverse is true of the very silent set; they cling to first-person choices from the beginning, with only a modest movement towards more third person uses as they get older.

Explanation is synonymous with speculation in a situation like this, but one plausible hypothesis suggests itself. Membership of these extreme groups was determined by the reluctance or otherwise of pupils to engage freely in talk with the children or adults in their class-room lives. If their view of the world is to be reflected in their writing, the very silent would be likely to put 'I' at the centre as a kind of com-posite speaker-hearer. The very talkative, in contrast, would value an external audience, 'they', more highly.

If this is more than a temporary phase in development, the implica-tions are worth pondering. Which of the two groups is the more likely to adapt to the demands of impersonal transactional writing? Does one group have an advantage over the other in developing the poetic function from the expressive? Will the very silent be relatively insensi-tive to the response of audience? Is some teaching action called for, and what form might it take? There are no sure answers to these ques-tions, because the information is too sketchy and uncertain, but this example reinforces a recurring plea in this book that we need to know much more about writers and their writing if our teaching is to become more coherently productive. The search for greater understanding is our collective responsibility.

9

Conclusion and Prospect

'True ease in writing comes from art, not chance,
As those move easiest who have learned to dance'
(Alexander Pope – *An Essay on Criticism*)

'If, as I believe, writing is learned in the same basic way other activities
are learned – by doing and by heeding what happens – then it is possible
to describe ideal teaching practice in this way and compare them with
some current methods.'
(James Moffett – *Teaching the Universe of Discourse*)

To employ a term like 'conclusion' is to import suggestions of finality
and completeness; a full-stop when a comma would be more accurate.
In an earlier analogy, this enterprise was compared with a contribution
to map-making, adding a few new features, revising some old ones,
suggesting alternative approaches to the map's interpretation. The map
remains incomplete, not just because no enquiry could hope to encompass all its detail, but because the country it describes is constantly
changing.

In historical perspective, the early years of the 1970s may well seem
a period of marking time in the teaching of writing, after the rich but
wayward energy of the creative writing era had been all but exhausted.
The publication of the Bullock Report and the gathering momentum
of the drive to secure fuller adult literacy are perhaps signs that the
time is ripe for the next development, but experience shows that there
is no way of legislating for it. Writing is still dominated by reading;
literacy for most people invokes the first 'R', with concern for writing
a very distant second. If the full force of the argument for writing is
accepted, these two modes of language use need to be taken together,
as equal and complementary processes. The apparent surface restrictions to the utility of writing in a technological society cover its deeper
values; its role in facilitating and shaping thought and Vygotsky's
claim for its power in aiding speech development.

The forces acting on educational practice in any period are never easily disentangled, least of all by an observer within the time under scrutiny. Working against a more exalted position for writing it is possible to list the belief in a decline in the reign of print before the irresistible advance of audio-visual media. New movements in linguistics have rightly asserted the primacy of speech. Much of the exploratory research into ways of learning and teaching is now directed at the processes of verbal (i.e. oral) interaction and at the part to be played by technology in education. While the drive for universal reading competence is strong, it has a notably functional air and writing, its productive counterpart, is left to take care of itself. To redress the balance somewhat, the Schools Council has sponsored two major enquiries into writing at secondary school level: James Britton's investigation of the development of writing abilities, 11–18, and the work of Nancy Martin on writing across the curriculum, 11–13. Writing's primary school beginnings have tended to be taken for granted.

The overriding theme of this book, on which all the detailed arguments and expositions converge, is summarised in the quotations which open this chapter. Writing skill will grow with practice, but if there are no guiding principles informing the setting and the response, any growth will depend for its speed and strength on the uncertain operation of our intentions as teachers. No return to the rigidities of earlier methods of writing instruction is implied; as Moffett points out, doing and heeding what happens are natural, basic ways of learning. Our function is to make use of all the knowledge we possess of the process of learning to write, in order to help children to do the appropriate things in the most effective order and to equip them to understand and learn from what happens when they write. A concern for purpose and audience, for patterns of development in language mastery, for the effects of context on writing, for the treatment of writing and action to ease the learner's difficulties, is the foundation on which a policy for writing may be elaborated with some confidence.

And yet the map is incomplete. Each enquiry adds a little to the sum of understanding of what happens when pen meets paper but, as those who have tried it will know only too well, for each question apparently answered, ten appear to take its place. This is no argument for rejecting the understanding that has been accumulated, but it does counsel caution in its acceptance. Our project dug quite deeply into one aspect of the language children command in writing, but left huge areas unexplored. In trying to explain why individual children perform as they do, the limitations of our understanding of them becomes all too clear, as the examples of the preceding chapter illustrated. The implications, if any, of those unusual patterns of pronoun use remain a mystery. Other major questions were left out of consideration because there was no time to engage with them, despite the four years over which the enquiry extended.

So it is full circle back to the starting point; a group of teachers defining a question and pursuing an answer to it – other teachers, other questions than those explored here. With teachers' centres now widely and successfully established, the opportunities for teacher-initiated enquiries on this or similar lines are much enhanced. Enthusiasts should take heed of our painfully-acquired experience, though; any question will take three times as long to explore as you first estimated. A selection of our unanswered questions is offered for consideration:

(1) What is the relationship between the quality of a piece of writing and the range of language resources employed to produce it?
(2) How does skill in speaking relate to skill in writing? How does one explain the frequent disparities between them?
(3) What is there to be learnt about the effects of physical setting on writing?
(4) What are the writing expectations of secondary-school teachers for incoming pupils? How realistic are they, related to the developmental level of the children concerned?
(5) How far is it possible to describe in detail how junior-school pupils move out from the 'expressive' function to 'transactional' and 'poetic'? Are there definable transitional steps?
(6) What effective ways are there of helping the non-progressing child through his difficulties?
(7) Are there productive methods for encouraging children to extend their syntactic resources (e.g. by sentence-combining) which do not carry the danger of degenerating into empty exercises?

I will borrow 8-year-old Christine's final sentence for my own:

'I am tried of writting this long story so this is truely THE END.'

Bibliography

Abbs, P., *Creating for Ourselves* in Approaches series (London, Heinemann Educational, 1974).

Albrow, K. H., *The English Writing System*, Papers in Linguistics and English Teaching, Series II (London, Longman, 1974).

Applebee, R. K., 'The Transatlantic Dialogue' in N. Bagnall (ed.), *New Movements in the Study and Teaching of English* (London, Temple-Smith, 1973).

Armitstead, P., *English in the Middle Years* (Oxford, Blackwell, 1972).

Arnold, M., *Reports on Elementary Schools 1852–1882* (London, HMSO, 1908).

Ashworth, E., *Language in the Junior School* (London, Edward Arnold, 1973).

Beckett, J., *The Keen Edge* (London, Blackie, 1965).

Bernstein, B., *Class, Codes, Control*, Vols 1 and 2 (London, Routledge & Kegan Paul, 1971, 1973).

Blackie, J., *Good Enough for the Children?* (London, Faber, 1963).

Bloomfield, L., *Language* (London, George Allen & Unwin, 1934).

Bolt, S. F., *The Right Response* (London, Hutchinson Educational, 1966).

Boyd, W., 'The Development of Sentence Structure in Childhood', *Brit. J. Psychol.* 17, 3 (1927).

Braddock, R., Lloyd-Jones, R., Schoer, L., *Research in Written Composition* (Champaign, Illinois, NCTE, 1963).

Brimer, M. A., Dunn, L. M., *Manual for the English Picture Vocabulary Tests* (Bristol, Educ. Evaluation Enterprises, 1962).

Britton, J. N. (ed.), *Talking and Writing* (London, Methuen, 1967).

Britton, J. N., in *Explorations in Children's Writing*, E. L. Evertts (ed.) (Champaign, Illinois, NCTE, 1970).

Britton, J. N., *Language and Learning* (Harmondsworth, Allen Lane, The Penguin Press, 1970).

Brooks, C., Warren, R. P., *Fundamentals of Good Writing – a Handbook of Modern Rhetoric* (London, Dennis Dobson, 1952).

Bullock, Sir A., *A Language for Life* (London, HMSO, 1975).

Burgess, T. *et al., Understanding Children Writing* (Harmondsworth, Penguin Education, 1973).

Burroughs, G. E. R., *A Study of the Vocabulary of Young Children* (Birmingham University Institute of Education, Ed. Monographs 1, Oliver & Boyd, 1957).

Burrows, A. T. *et al., They All Want to Write*, rev. edn (New York, Prentice-Hall, 1952).

Chomsky, C., *The Acquisition of Syntax in Children from 5 to 10* (Cambridge, Mass., MIT Press, 1969).

Chomsky, N., *Aspects of the Theory of Syntax* (Cambridge, Mass., MIT Press, 1965).

Clegg, A. B. (ed.), *The Excitement of Writing* (London, Chatto & Windus, 1964).

Clements, S., Dixon, J., Stratta L., *Reflections* (London, Oxford University Press, 1963).

Coulthard, M., 'A Discussion of Restricted and Elaborated Codes', *Educ. Review* 22, 1 (1969).

Crowther, Sir G., *15 to 18, Vol. I*, Report of the Central Advisory Council for Education (London, HMSO, 1959).

Dewey, J., *How We Think*, rev. edn (Boston, D. C. Heath, 1933).

Dixon, J., *Growth through English* (Reading, NATE, 1967).

Dixon, P., *The Critical Idiom: Rhetoric* (London, Methuen, 1971).

Doughty, P., Pearce, J., Thornton, G. M., *Language in Use* (London, Edward Arnold, 1971).

Doughty, P., Pearce, J., Thornton, G. M., *Exploring Language* (London, Edward Arnold, 1972).

Douglas, J. W. B., *The Home and the School* (London, MacGibbon & Kee, 1964).

Druce, R., *The Eye of Innocence* (London, Brockhampton Press, 1965).

Faraday, M., *The Chemical History of a Candle* (London, Scientific Book Guild, 1960).

Fletcher, H., Howell, A., *Mathematics for Schools* (London, Addison-Wesley, 1972).

Fraser, H., *Control and Create* (London, Longman, 1967).

Fraser, H., O'Donnell, W. (eds.), *Applied Linguistics and the Teaching of English* (London, Longman, 1969).

Ginsburg, H., Opper, S., *Piaget's Theory of Intellectual Development* (New Jersey, Prentice-Hall, 1969).

Goody, J. (ed.), *Literacy in Traditional Societies* (Cambridge, Cambridge University Press, 1968).

Gordon, V. E. C., Mock, R., *Twentieth Century Handwriting* (London, Methuen, 1960).

Gregson, J. M., *English-Schooling in the Middle Years* (London, Macmillan, 1973).

Grierson, H. J. C., *Rhetoric and English Composition*, 2nd edn (Edinburgh, Oliver & Boyd, 1945).

Hadow, Sir W. H., Report of the Consultative Committee on the Primary School (London, HMSO, 1931).

Haggitt, T. W., *Working with Language* (Oxford, Blackwell, 1967).

Halliday, M. A. K., 'Language Structure and Language Function', in J. Lyons (ed.), *New Horizons in Linguistics* (Harmondsworth, Penguin, 1970).

Halliday, M. A. K., 'Foreword' in B. Bernstein (ed.), *Class, Codes and Control*, Vol. 2 (London, Routledge & Kegan Paul, 1973).

Halliday, M. A. K., McIntosh, A., Strevens, P., *The Linguistic Sciences and Language Teaching* (London, Longman, 1964).

Hanna, P. R., Hanna, J. S., *Phoneme-Grapheme Correspondence as Cues to Spelling Improvement* (Washington, US Office of Education, 1966).

Harpin, W. S. *et al.*, *Social and Educational Influences on Children's Acquisition of Grammar* (SSRC Research Report, 757, 1973).

Harrell, L. E., 'A Comparison of the Development of Oral and Written Language in School Age Children', *Society for Research in Child Development* XXII, 3 (1957).

Hawkins, P. R., 'Social Class, the Nominal Group and Reference', *Language and Speech*, 12, 2 (1969).

Hitchfield, E. M., *In Search of Promise*, Studies in Child Development (London, Longman with the National Children's Bureau, 1973).

Holbrook, D., *English for the Rejected* (Cambridge, Cambridge University Press, 1964).

Holbrook, D., *Children's Writing* (Cambridge, Cambridge University Press, 1967).

Holt, J., *How Children Fail* (London, Pitman, 1964).

Hourd, M. L., *The Education of the Poetic Spirit* (London, Heinemann, 1949).

Hourd, M. L., Cooper, G. E., *Coming into Their Own* (London, Heinemann, 1959).

Hunt, K. W., *Grammatical Structures Written at Three Grade Levels* (Champaign, Illinois, NCTE Research Report 3, 1965).

Jeremiah, T. G., *A Source Book of Creative Themes* (Oxford, Blackwell, 1972).

Joos, M., *The Five Clocks* (Indiana, Indiana University Press, 1962).

Joos, M., in Funk, H. D., and Triplett, D. (eds), *Language Arts in the Elementary School: Readings* (Philadelphia, Lippincott, 1972).

Labov, W., 'The Logic of Non-Standard English', abridged in P. P. Giglioli (ed.), *Language and Social Context* (Harmondsworth, Penguin, 1972).

La Brant, L. L., 'A Study of Certain Language Developments in Children', *Genet. Psychol. Monographs*, 14 (1933).

Lane, S. M., Kemp, M., *An Approach to Creative Writing in the Primary School* (London, Blackie, 1967).

Langdon, M., *Let the Children Write* (London, Longman, 1961).

Lawton, D., *Social Class, Language and Education* (London, Routledge & Kegan Paul, 1968).

Leech, G. N., *A Linguistic Guide to English Poetry* (London, Longman, 1969).

Loban, W. D., *The Language of Elementary School Children* (Champaign, Illinois, NCTE Research Report 1, 1963).

McCarthy, D. A., 'Language Development in Children', in L. Carmichael (ed.), *Manual of Child Psychology*, 2nd edn (New York, Wiley, 1954).

Mackay, D. D., Thompson B., Schaub, P., *Breakthrough to Literacy – Teacher's Manual* (London, Longman, 1972).

McLuhan, M., *The Gutenberg Galaxy* (London, Routledge & Kegan Paul, 1962).

McNally J., Murray, W., *Key Words to Literacy* (London, Schoolmaster Pub. Co., 1962).

McNeill, D., *The Acquisition of Language* (New York, Harper and Row, 1970).

Martin, N. C., 'What Are They up to?' in A. Jones and J. Mulford, *Children Using Language* (Oxford, NATE, Oxford University Press, 1971).

Martin, N. C. *et al.*, 'Why?', 'From Talking to Writing', 'Keeping Options Open', 'From Information to Understanding', 'Writing in Science', pamphlets produced for the *Writing Across the Curriculum, 11–31 Project* (Schools Council and London University Institute of Education, 1973, 1974).

Mattam, D., *The Vital Approach*, 2nd edn (Oxford, Pergamon, 1973).

Maybury, B., *Creative Writing for Juniors* (London, Batsford, 1967).

Mellon, J., *Transformational Sentence-Combining: A Method of Enhancing the Development of Syntactic Fluency in English Composition* (Harvard Research Project, US Office of Education, 1966).

Ministry of Education, *Language – Some Suggestions for Teachers of English and Others* (London, HMSO, 1954).

Ministry of Education, *Early Leaving*, Central Advisory Council for Education (England) (London, HMSO, 1954).

Moffett, J., *Teaching the Universe of Discourse* (Boston, Houghton Mifflin, 1968).

Nesfield, J. C., *Manual of English Grammar and Composition*, 2nd edn (London, Macmillan, 1922).

Newbolt, H. *et al.*, *The Teaching of English in England* (London, HMSO, 1921).

Peel, M., *Seeing to the Heart* (London, Chatto & Windus, 1967).

Peters, M. L., *Spelling: Caught or Taught?* (London, Routledge & Kegan Paul, 1967).

Peters, M. L., in Wade, B., Wedell, K. (eds), *Spelling: Task and Learner* (Birmingham, Educational Review Occasional Publications 5, 1974).

Plowden, Lady B., *Children and Their Primary Schools*, Vol. 1 (London, HMSO, 1967).

Postman, N., 'The Politics of Reading' in N. Keddie (ed.), *Tinker, Tailor . . . The Myth of Cultural Deprivation* (Harmondsworth, Penguin, 1973).

Pym, D., *Free Writing* (University of Bristol Publication No. 10, University of London Press, 1954).

Quirk, R., *The Use of English*, 2nd edn (London, Longmans, 1968).

Rance, P., *Teaching by Topics* (London, Ward Lock Educational, 1968).

Raven, J. C., *Guide to the Standard Progressive Matrices* (London, H. K. Lewis, 1960).

Raven, J. C., *Guide to Using the Coloured Progressive Matrices* (London, H. K. Lewis, 1963).

Read, H., Dobrée, B., *The London Book of English Prose* (London, Eyre & Spottiswoode, 1960).

Rinsland, H. D., *A Basic Vocabulary of Elementary School Children* (New York, Macmillan, 1945).

Robbins, Lord, *Higher Education* (London, HMSO, 1963).

Roberts, G., *English in Primary Schools* (London, Routledge & Kegan Paul, 1972).

Rosen, H., *Language and Class* (Bristol, Falling Wall Press, 1972).

Sampson, G., *English for the English* (Cambridge, Cambridge University Press, 1921).

Schonell, F. J., *Backwardness in the Basic Subjects*, 4th edn (Edinburgh, Oliver & Boyd, 1948).

Stott, D. H., *The Social Adjustment of Children*, 3rd edn (London, University of London Press, 1966).

Stratta, L., Dixon, J., Wilkinson, A., *Patterns of Language* (London, Heinemann Educational, 1973).

Sutton, C., 'Language and Communication in Science Lessons' in *The Art of the Science Teacher* (Science Teacher Education Project, McGraw-Hill, 1974).

Taylor, J., *Reading and Writing in the First School* (London, George Allen & Unwin, 1973).

Templin, M., in Smith F., Miller G. A. (eds), *The Genesis of Language* (Cambridge, Mass., MIT Press, 1966).

Thomson, J. A. K., *Classical Influences on English Prose* (London, George Allen & Unwin, 1956).

Thorndike, E. L., Lorge, I., *The Teacher's Word Book*, rev. edn (New York, Teachers' College, Columbia University, 1931).

Thorndike, E. L., Evans, A., Kennon, L. H., Newcomb, E. I., 'An Inventory of English Constructions', *Teacher's College Records*, 28 (1926–7).

Tucker, B., *Teaching English in the Middle Years* (London, Ward Lock Educational, 1973).

Vygotsky, L. S., *Thought and Language* (Cambridge, Mass., MIT Press, 1962).

Weir, R., *Language in the Crib* (The Hague, Mouton, 1962).

Wilkinson, A. *et al., Spoken English* (Birmingham Educational Review Occasional Publications 2, 1965).

Yeats, W. B., *Selected Poetry*, Jeffares, N. (ed.) (London, Macmillan, 1962).

Index

personal pronoun use 60, 61, 75, 79, 123, 154
Peters, M. L. 133, 152
phatic communion 33
photography 100, 116
Piaget, J. 70, 114–16
picture sequences 106
Poetry writing 29
Pope, Alexander 145, 155
Postman, N. 21
preparation for writing 135–7
pre-writing activities 126
project work 101
punctuation 57, 67, 131–2, 134–5, 152
Pym, D. 27, 105

Quirk, R. 129
quotation 119

Rance, P. 118
Raven's Matrices 75
Read, H., Dobrée B. 41
reading and writing 22, 30, 112–13, 116–17, 140, 150, 152
reading skills 113
register 40
Registrar-General's classification 78
'rehearsal' for writing 121, 135, 137
relative pronoun 71–2
research design 19–20
research in teaching 16, 17
research objectives 18–19, 157
review 102
Revised Code 23
rhetoric 36–7
Rinsland, H. D. 55
Roberts, G. 105

Sampson, G. 25
Schonell, F. J. 63–4,67
Schools Council 16, 156
sentence, identification of 57, 59; kinds of 57–8
sex differences 54, 60, 74–5
social development 115
Social Science Research Council 18
speech 25, 26, 51, 78, 136; as creative process 53; example from John (4) 68
spelling 67, 131–4, 152
standards in English 29

stimuli for writing 27, 93–5, 117–18, 145, 146
Stott, D. H. 81
Stratta, L., Dixon, J., Wilkinson, A. 109
styles in language 39
subjects for writing 92–3
subordinate clause, common and uncommon 60, 61, 62, 69
subordination, index of 59, 61, 75; kinds of 69–70
summary 101, 118
Sutton, C. 104

talkativeness and silence 153–4
tape-recording 108, 150
Taylor, J. 117
teacher expectations 46, 93, 95, 109, 133, 140
teachers and teaching methods 16, 26, 27, 92, 108–10, 111–12, 128–9, 133–4, 151–2, 154, 155–6
television 55, 102, 104, 108
Templin, M. C. 75
Thomson, J. A. K. 41
Thorndike, E. L. 55, 59
Three Rs 23, 155
topic, project, centre of interest 118–19
Tucker, B. 117
T unit 59
type-token ratio (T.T.R.) 56

vernacular in schools 22
vocabulary 54–6, 128, 130
Vygotsky, L. 52–3, 155

Weir, R. 139
Wilkinson, A. 17
word, as grammatical unit 57
word count 53–4
Writing across the Curriculum Project 92, 156
writing, 'average' 63–7, 145–6; and audience 35, 37, 39–40, 41, 45, 92, 122, 140–1, 149; and family size, birth order 82–3; and handedness 83–4, 126; and measured ability 75–7; and print 21–2; and social adjustment 81–2, 145, 147; and social class membership 76, 77–80; and speech